THE MOVIE
MAKERS **BOGART**

BOGART

Allen Eyles

M

Front Endpaper: *Key Largo*
Back Endpaper: *The*
Petrified Forest
Half-title: *The Left Hand*
of God
Title page: *Casablanca*

SBN 333 18020 8

First published 1975 by
Macmillan London Limited
London and Basingstoke
Associated companies in New York, Toronto,
Dublin, Melbourne, Johannesburg and Delhi

Printed in Great Britain
by Jolly & Barber Ltd., Rugby
Bound by Dorstel Press Ltd., Harlow

Contents

1.THE MAKING
OF THE LEGEND

When Humphrey Bogart died, on 14 January 1957, circumstances gave a special twist to the sad news that made headlines around the world. Bogart was barely past his mid-fifties, still active, in heavy demand, very nearly as popular as he had ever been and busily broadening his appeal with more varied roles than before. Our loss was not only that of the man but the films he would have undoubtedly gone on to make. Then there was the nature of his death. His courageous, painful, protracted battle with cancer – long hinted at, confirmed in detail after the announcement of his death – evoked admiration and respect, and attached the screen image of bravery to the man himself. Furthermore, of the great stars who had sprung up in the thirties and forties to become Hollywood's 'immortals', Bogart was the first to go. In the years preceding his death, only James Dean's demise had caused anything like an equivalent stir, and that was a special case; otherwise, John Garfield was the biggest loss, but that was much earlier and he was mourned less. After Bogart, death pounced on Gable, Cooper, Tyrone Power, Alan Ladd . . . causing the same jolt of realization about the mortality of their flesh until their immortality on celluloid asserted itself again.

None of these factors weigh much beside the consideration that Bogart *deserves* to be remembered for the uncommonly fine and sensitive actor he was. It is not necessary to embrace the simple-minded adulation of the camp crowd and the cult-makers to respond warmly to his particular qualities as a performer and to find a topical relevance in his style.

Of course, luck played its part. Though stardom came late to Bogart, it gave him a good number of great films in which to develop and display his persona to great effect. (If Alan Ladd had managed a few more films like *Shane*, if Gable had come up with a few more like *Gone with the Wind* and *It Happened One Night*, then they might match Bogart's place in popular affection.) Bogart has *The Maltese Falcon, Casablanca, The Big Sleep, Dark Passage, In a Lonely Place, The Treasure of the Sierra Madre, The African Queen* and others, their greatness inextricably attached to Bogart's own contribution to them. With another actor, each would have been another film – and, it's surely safe to say, one nowhere near as good.

The public is very selective about what it responds to and prizes from the past. Mostly, and understandably, it is the great laughter-makers who are warmly appreciated today: Keaton, the Marx Brothers, Fields, Laurel and Hardy, Chaplin. But at other times, for other moods, there is a need for the fragility of Garbo, the brashness of Cagney – and the stoic heroism of Bogart.

Bogart is usually a man confronted by danger. His many gangster films of the thirties, in which he died in the last reel, for ever stamped him as a vulnerable figure who could very possibly die before the end. These early criminal psychopaths

A portrait of Humphrey Bogart, in costume for *The Left Hand of God* (1955). Eighteen months later he was dead

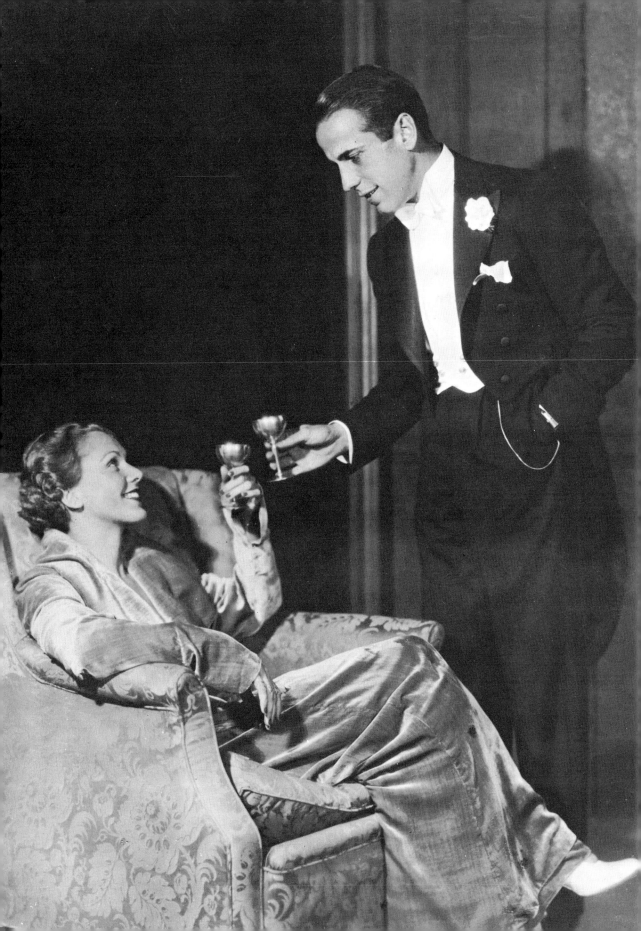

also marked him later as a man of volatile temperament and violent inner impulses. Many of Bogart's films are as much concerned with inner stress as with outside danger; and in any case it is the style of his response to events that takes our attention.

His neurotic touchiness (in real life, he hated strangers to lay a hand on him) and his clammed-up aloofness seem to reflect a profound disillusionment and disenchantment. It is events that have made the screen Bogart the way he is, and so he has our sympathy rather than our condemnation for his faults of character.

In the forties Bogart, one senses a craving for emotional honesty and deep commitment, for a place to safely repose a battered trust. He is a misanthropist in search of a cause, a misogynist awaiting only the right woman. Often there are no happy solutions to his problems, only more living to be done with as much style as possible. Bogart's is thus an intensely modern dilemma. He is a model hero for our muddled and dangerous times.

His particular effectiveness as a screen performer begins with his looks. Photographs of him as a Broadway juvenile in the twenties are hard to believe: they show a striking smile, a lean face and well-oiled hair in the Valentino tradition. He had debonair, uncomplicated looks that suited his lightweight roles in romantic comedy. That noted actress Louise Brooks has recalled the Bogart she knew in 1924 as a slim, quiet, charming man, his handsome features given a fascinating touch by a loose piece of skin hanging from his upper lip: a result of a wound while in the Navy. She declares that he only had 'this endearing disfigurement' patched up when he went into films and, furthermore, that it gave him no speech impediment at all.

That good-looking Bogart with the stitched upper lip went to Hollywood in the early thirties and vied unsuccessfully with all the other good-looking young men who could remember lines, articulate clearly, swing a tennis racket and sip a cocktail. It was not until *The Petrified Forest* (1936) that Bogart made an impression – an indelible one of a man who has taken a lot of wear and tear. The Bogart face now had 'character', had experienced life and was hardened by most of what it had seen.

This was the image Bogart worked on. He played up his facial aberrations – the twitch in the right cheek at moments of stress or annoyance, the unusually moist lower lip that gleamed under the lights, the watery eyes that also glittered vividly – and made it a face to watch. He told cameramen like James Wong Howe: 'Don't take the lines out of my face. Leave them there.' In *Dark Passage* (1947) he allowed his features to be passed off as the result of plastic surgery, and in his own production of *In a Lonely Place* (1950) he joked about his

Bogart as a Broadway juvenile in the twenties: the play and the actress are unidentified

appearance by responding to Gloria Grahame's suggestion that he has an interesting face by looking in the mirror and remarking, 'How could anybody like a face like this?' 'I said I liked it, I didn't say I wanted to kiss it,' Grahame replies, putting Bogart in his place. In fact Ingrid Bergman had to vouch to a dubious Jack Warner for Bogart's sex appeal before he was definitely assigned to *Casablanca* (1942).

In the film that started him off on leading roles in major films and the attendant romantic opportunities, *The Maltese Falcon*(1941), he apparently dispensed with all makeup, as he did, very evidently, years later for *The Treasure of the Sierra Madre* (1948). In one startling image, the dusty hobo rises from the chair of a Tampico barber's shop looking like a cleaned-up cadaver with his hair (actually a toupée) slicked down and his bony forehead jutting out. Equally bold and devastating was the filthy ruin he allowed himself to become in *The African Queen* (1952) with his stained shirt, stubbled chin and unruly stomach.

Bogart had his vain side. If the part didn't require the opposite, he did like to dress smartly in later years and nearly always sported a bow tie from *Tokyo Joe* (1949) onwards, while in that most appearance-conscious of films, *Beat the Devil*(1953), he is shown selecting and fastening his neckwear. Though he allowed himself to be photographed off set with thinning hair in the mid-1940s, he subsequently vetoed shots that did not include his hairpiece in place. But Bogart appreciated the value of a distinctive face and there must have been times when the conventional goodlookers like Robert Taylor and Alan Ladd gazed at him in envy. Critics who remarked on the breakthrough of actors like Tom Courtenay and Dustin Hoffman who lacked conventional good looks had evidently forgotten all about Bogart.

Bogart's voice was unusual too, with its slight lisp. Booming in *The Petrified Forest*, coarse in this and other early roles where his dialogue was of the 'dis', 'dat' and 'dose' variety, it was never comfortable donning an accent (though off screen Bogart was reputedly a brilliant mimic of such fellow players as Sydney Greenstreet). The speech impediment was no impediment at all: Bogart spoke cleanly, fast, forcefully – sometimes at a dizzy pace as when tearing into the D.A. in *The Maltese Falcon*, pausing considerately to inquire whether the stenographer was keeping up (and showing it was all an act).

Bogart was also one of the great men with a cigarette. It gave his hands a prop to work with. He would hang it distinctively from the right hand corner of his mouth to await a light. It is there as he emerges from the drab apartment block in *The Harder They Fall* (1956), so that he can pause to light it before striding forward and thereby make a strong first appearance in the film. In *The Big Sleep* (1946), he makes a phone call from a hamburger joint and pauses to go across for a light from the girl on the counter, solely to bring on the latest in the long succession of glamorous women he runs across in that film. In *The Maltese Falcon*, Bogart smartly divests Peter Lorre's Joel Cairo of his pointed gun, slaps him on to the sofa (after pausing very briefly for the audience to relish Cairo's imminent come-uppance), and all the while retains the cigarette in his mouth. He humiliates Wilmer (Elisha Cook Jr.) by blowing a stream of cigarette smoke into his face and having him removed from the hotel lobby. In *Casablanca* (1942) the haze of cigarette smoke around his melancholy figure helps blur the image into the flashback sequence.

Bogart was the antithesis of the deadpan, laconic, ambling, or hearty kind of screen hero. He was a nervous, hypersensitive figure. His face was like a seismograph recording the release of energy elsewhere and his features would crease up alarmingly with any kind of routine physical exertion like packing a suitcase or reaching down to tie a shoelace. It was only to be expected that his gangsters would behave in a violent, unpredictable way, but his later roles seemed to retain some of this anger, waiting to be triggered off. When Bogart exploded, the display was truly frightening.

In *The Maltese Falcon* he throws a fit of temper to make an impression on Sydney Greenstreet's Fat Man and walks out

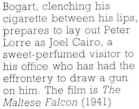

Bogart, clenching his cigarette between his lips, prepares to lay out Peter Lorre as Joel Cairo, a sweet-perfumed visitor to his office who has had the effrontery to draw a gun on him. The film is *The Maltese Falcon* (1941)

on him; in the corridor outside his room, Bogart grins to himself and glances at his hands which are still shaking from the energy he has poured into his act. Real anger is no different: after he has shot one of the Vichy French in *To Have and Have Not* (1944), he holds the rest at gunpoint and has to transfer his weapon from one hand to the other since he is trembling so much. His look indicates to the surviving villains just how near they came to being shot as well. In *The Big Sleep* (1946), Bogart confronts Eddie Mars (John Ridgely) and terrifies the cold-blooded killer into being blasted to death by his own men in the ambush he planned to spring on Bogart. The urgency in Bogart's voice, the shots he fires at Eddie, are convincing reasons for Eddie to take his chances outside. Bogart's heavy breathing as he telephones the police indicate how much nervous energy he has put into the confrontation, knowingly placing himself in Eddie's trap with only the advantage of surprise and his gun to extricate himself.

During *In a Lonely Place* (1950), only the twitch in his right cheek betrays his rising anger with the man who is teasing a friend before he turns and punches the bully to the floor. Here the violence is all the more disturbing, coming from a man who is a writer by profession. In that same film, the way Bogart's hands vibrate as he tries to light a cigarette are an alarming

Bogart, 'looking like a cleaned-up cadaver', in discussion with his favourite director, John Huston, during production of *The Treasure of the Sierra Madre* (1948). Huston is wearing the white suit for an appearance in the film as an American tourist from whom Bogart, as a down-and-out in Tampico, repeatedly seeks a hand-out

expression of his mental agitation as he realizes he is being betrayed by the woman he loves.

Even smaller gestures could enhance a film. Bogart's 'involuntary' grimace of dislike for his former mistress (played by Gladys George) when her back is turned always delights audiences watching *The Maltese Falcon*. Then there is the moment in *In a Lonely Place* when two old ladies interrupt his conversation in a restaurant, looking for a book of matches as a souvenir of their visit, and Bogart nods to himself with faint amusement; another touch that colours a part, making the Bogart character that much more real and convincingly human.

But it was not only the incidental or sharp reaction – like his tight-lipped disgust with his partner James Cagney's high-handed behaviour in *The Roaring Twenties* (1939), which prompts him to reach for the phone to arrange his early demise – that Bogart conveyed. There was also the deep-seated feeling that leads him masochistically to revive old emotional torments in *Casablanca*.

Bogart's actions and reactions were usually carefully considered; only under extreme provocation did he blow his top. One of the more atypical but extraordinary and appealing moments in his entire career is that in *The African Queen* when, after the frail vessel has survived a barrage of German bullets and a hazardous descent through some rapids, Bogart tosses away Katharine Hepburn's hat and seizes her for a jubilant kiss. But so expansive a gesture is frowned upon by many Bogart admirers, who find it undignified.

Bogart was skilled in the art of listening. He knew how to ensure that you noticed he was listening as much as you noticed what other players were saying. In *The Big Sleep*, he developed a mannerism of fingering his right ear lobe thoughtfully – an understandable response to the daunting complexities of the plot – and this was a device among many, seen in other films without the same emphasis or frequency of use. He was employing it as early as *China Clipper* (1936). He and Ross Alexander are on equal pegging as characters and have separate close-ups seated in a classroom. Ross Alexander just listens; Bogart listens and toys with his ear. In *The Maltese Falcon*, Bogart sits beside Mary Astor taking in her lies of the day. His finger thoughtfully brushes his lower lip. At other times, in this and other pictures, Bogart would stroke his forehead, pinch his nose, rub his chin and do all manner of physical tricks that seem spontaneous and accidental but cannot have been anything of the sort in the very deliberate and calculated atmosphere of film-making. It would be wrong to exaggerate this aspect of Bogart's craft, or to suggest that other actors didn't practise the same devices, but they were part of Bogart's particular alertness and depth as a performer, lending substance to his basic screen magnetism.

2.THE REAL BOGART

ogart's private life further added to his lustre as a movie star. The actor was very publicity conscious and knew full well that colourful articles in the newspapers enhanced his commercial value. Many of his best friends were members of the press, past and present, and he even gave some columnists direct access to him without an appointment. The press in turn liked Bogart because he could be relied upon to provide stimulating views on almost any subject and show disrespect towards some of Hollywood's sacred cows.

Though Bogart was reportedly something of a prankster during his acting days on Broadway, he married twice during the twenties without causing a great stir and lived uneventfully in Hollywood in the early thirties. Louise Brooks, in *Sight and Sound* (Winter 1966/67), suggests that, having been a serious actor who had not been very successful and had failed one chance in Hollywood, he was only too keen to promote himself once he tasted success with *The Petrified Forest*. At any rate, Bogart provided Hollywood with the colourful spectacle of incessant public feuding with his temperamental third wife, Mayo Methot (whose quirky facial expressions as a supporting actress in such thirties films as *Mr Deeds Goes to Town* may have inspired the facial mannerisms of her husband). Subsequently, Bogart provided a classic case of a popular headline romance when he fell for and married Lauren Bacall, thereby also rejuvenating his screen image.

Clearly, Bogart did prize his Hollywood success and the life style it made possible. When he came to Hollywood to film *The Petrified Forest*, it was a one-way trip; he never went back to the stage. By 1940 he was quite unapologetic about leaving it behind, invoking the responsibilities he had towards his mother and two younger sisters (his father had died). At that time he professed ambitions to become a film director, as though foreseeing a limited run as a player in Hollywood; later, when he could have directed, he seems to have given up the idea.

Despite his well-publicized off-screen antics, Bogart took Hollywood and his work seriously. Like most stars who worked in the Warner Bros. film factory, he chafed at the parts he was given. In his case, they were either roles turned down by the studio's bigger stars – Cagney, Paul Muni, George Raft, Edward G. Robinson, Garfield – or else roles that these luminaries had already played that were now being cast in cheap B-feature re-makes. Bogart's frequent suspensions mostly postdated the more celebrated battles of Cagney, Bette Davis and Olivia de Havilland against the Brothers Warner; they were probably no more than routine procedure for gaining a salary adjustment and some useful publicity as a rebel or underdog.

Those who worked with Bogart have almost invariably attested to his professionalism as an actor. He came prepared

Bogart had a great love of the sea, and is seen here with his wife Lauren Bacall aboard his yawl, *Santana*

or could, if necessary, commit pages of script to memory in a matter of minutes. He disliked the improvisers, the people who had to work their way into feeling a scene, or the fifty-take perfectionists. Only rarely did Bogart's well-known love of the bottle interfere with his capacity to act. On *To Have and Have Not*, he was reprimanded by director Howard Hawks and quickly reformed. On *Passage to Marseille* (1944), cameraman James Wong Howe recalls that he arranged with Bogart to delay shooting for half an hour by fiddling around with the lights while the actor pulled himself together. Though Bogart liked to tease and needle people – especially those, like director Michael Curtiz, who were not renowned for their sense of humour – and some delays in production may have resulted, Bogart never let his work suffer.

In the year when he was the screen's highest paid actor, 1946, Bogart made his move for future security by signing a fifteen year contract with Warner Bros. on 29 December. A contract of that length broke most, perhaps all precedents and Bogart, according to legend, made Jack Warner feel faint at the image he painted of himself, going toothless and bald during the run of that marathon agreement. In the event, the contract was terminated in September 1953, when Bogart, who had script approval of his one annual film, found it increasingly difficult to find suitable properties belonging to the studio.

Bogart also sought to satisfy his craving for independence by going into production for himself. Directors had pioneered the idea and Bogart was one of the first stars to follow their example. He looked around for a partner with production experience and chose former newspaperman and drinking buddy Mark Hellinger, who had produced many of his Warner pictures in the early forties. Their films were to be released by David O. Selznick's newly formed distribution company. Then Hellinger suddenly died in December 1947, aged only forty-four. One of their projects had been to film *The Snows of Kilimanjaro*, with Jules Dassin directing, but the property was sold off on Hellinger's death to Fox, where it was made later.

Bogart then set up Santana Productions on 7 April 1948, naming the company after the 55-foot, 16-ton yawl he had bought and loved to sail during his spare time. He hired Robert Lord to work with him; like Hellinger he was an ex-newspaperman who had been a writer and producer at Warners while Bogart was there. In all, Santana made six films, for release by Columbia. Two of them, the mild comedy *And Baby Makes Three* (1949), and a forgettable drama, *The Silent Voice* (1951), were made without Bogart to establish the company as a bona fide production outfit as much as a personal tax saver.

On two of the other films Bogart worked with the young director Nicholas Ray and the results were artistically satisfying: one of the films, *Knock on Any Door* (1949), was a commercial success, the other, *In A Lonely Place* (1950), a box-office flop. The two remaining films, *Tokyo Joe* and *Sirocco* (1951), were undistinguished potboilers that turned in a solid profit. The company also helped set up *Beat the Devil* (1953) and was eventually sold to Columbia for one million dollars. One factor in Bogart's evident disillusionment with running a production company must have been his failure to outbid major studios for the kind of properties he wanted. Though he played in both *The Caine Mutiny* (1954) and *The Desperate Hours* (1955), he had initially been interested in buying their source material for himself.

Bogart also found it hard to express his political beliefs and maintain a good standing in Hollywood, as he was an ardent Democrat and liberal. When the House Un-American Activities Committee was conducting its notorious investigations in 1947, he joined the Committee of the First Amendment which was created by such figures as John Huston, William Wyler and Philip Dunne to suggest to the American public that HUAC was infringing the right of free speech. A large Hollywood group flew to Washington to give a press conference with stops en route to air their views to local pressmen. Bogart was the most prominent actor among them and he was inevitably identified as the leader. Their mission backfired when the public began to think of them as defenders of Communism rather than democracy. Bogart himself was labelled a Communist sympathizer or Red. He became the target of heavy criticism and began stating publicly that the Washington trip had been a mistake. He wrote (or approved) an article headed 'I'm No Communist' which appeared in the American *Photoplay* of March 1948. In this, however, he still managed to criticize the methods of HUAC ('there was no necessity for . . . the dirtying of many good names with no right to speak in their own defense') and defend liberals as a group devoted to democracy.

Earlier in the 1940s, Bogart had openly expressed his admiration for Franklin D. Roosevelt. Even this was highly frowned upon by the largely right-wing Hollywood establishment. He wrote another article, 'I Stuck My Neck Out', for the *Saturday Evening Post* (10 February 1945), defending a mere actor's right to express a political opinion. In the 1952 Presidential campaign, Bogart became a strong supporter of Adlai Stevenson and critic of Eisenhower, which was enough to make the studio heads mutter about the damage they might inflict on his career. But Bogart was not subdued. It was an ingrained part of his nature to speak his mind and stir things up.

It is tempting to imagine that the Bogart personality was forged in some Dead End ghetto of rampant delinquency. Though Bogart made his own way from the age of seventeen, he started life with a silver spoon in his mouth and became an infant celebrity whose chubby features were recognized wherever good women's magazines were read.

3. BABY FOOD TO BROADWAY

When a man has become such a legend, it is only to be expected that some of the facts about his life should have been 'improved' to make more of an impression on the gullible public. Bogart himself admitted to inventing stories for the fun of it – like having a secret ambition to play bull fiddle (double bass viol) in an orchestra. 'That's all bull without the fiddle,' he was later to confess. *Current Biography*, in a 1942 sketch of the actor, was understandably cautious when it came to his hobbies and interests: 'It is reported that he likes to sketch and paint, to play the bull fiddle, and to make chessmen out of ivory. It is reported, too, that his favourite flower is the hibiscus.'

But perhaps the most endearingly suspect part of the Bogart legend is that 'Humphrey was a Christmas present to his parents' by contriving to arrive in this world on Christmas Day. Look at biographical listings on Bogart before he became famous and his birthdate is quite different. Warners' campaign book on *The Petrified Forest* concentrates on the sensational re-teaming of the two stars of *Of Human Bondage* – Leslie Howard and Bette Davis – and gives Bogart an outline biography far shorter than that provided for each of the four players billed ahead of him – clearly the studio was unaware of how much impact his appearance in that film would make. So there was no reason to doctor the details – and his date of birth is given as 23 January, 1899. Shortly after, the change took place. The 1937–38 edition of the industry reference book *Motion Picture Almanac* switches from that date in previous editions to the one which was to persist thereafter: 25 December 1900. Evidently the actor liked the idea: at any rate, he always gave out Christmas Day as his birthday, though he modified the year to 1899. Over the years, Bogart also gained an inch and a half in publicity material over what seems to have been his true height of 5 ft 9½ ins.

Bogart's parents lived in a large brownstone house at 245 W. 103rd St, in Manhattan: his father, Belmont DeForest Bogart, was a doctor in general practice in a wealthy area, while his mother, Maud (Maude?) Humphrey Bogart, was a famous magazine illustrator who earned enormous fees. Her career ate into the time she had for her son, who was often to tell reporters that he had respected rather than loved his mother. The baby was named Humphrey DeForest Bogart and largely cared for by the servants (four in all, mostly Irish). However, Mrs Bogart sketched her son as an infant and sold the ensuing portrait to a manufacturer of baby foods. Young Bogart's sweet and jolly features smiled at readers from advertisements in all the women's magazines.

A few years later, Bogart was sent to a private school. He was taken on trips by his father; they often went sailing and he developed a life-long passion for the sea. In 1909, Bogart was enrolled at the strictly-run Trinity School in New York City

Humphrey DeForest Bogart, aged two. His cherubic features sold baby food

where he was an undistinguished pupil. Then in 1917 he went to his father's alma mater, Phillips Andover Academy in Massachusetts. By the spring of 1918 he had been thrown out for failing to achieve a proper academic standard. Far more colourful explanations for Bogart's dismissal were, of course, to be featured in later biographical sketches, Bogart himself relating some lively pranks. Bogart then went off and enlisted in the navy, lying about his age, and spent two years as a seaman, mainly crossing the Atlantic on troop carriers. During a U-boat attack, an exploding shell left a piece of shrapnel in Bogart's upper lip – or so one of the most familiar stories of Bogart's early life goes. However, Richard Gehman's biography of Bogart obtains from Bogart's brother-in-law the information that the wound was caused when Bogart was escorting a prisoner between naval bases and was hit in the face by the man's handcuffed hands, causing Bogart to shoot and wound his prisoner in self-defence.

Honourably discharged from the navy, Bogart dallied with a desk job for a shipping company (or was it freight-checking with the railroad?) and ran for a firm of Wall Street brokers. Then a long-standing friendship with Bill Brady Jr, whose father, a celebrated Broadway producer, lived on the same street, introduced Bogart to work in the theatre – and film. For Brady was venturing into film production at Fort Lee, New Jersey, and made Bogart an office boy in his company, World Films. During production of a Nita Naldi drama, *Life* (1920), the impresario quarrelled with director Travers Vale and sat Bogart in the director's chair to finish the picture. Not unexpectedly, the young man floundered and Brady himself took over. (You can believe that improbable story if you wish to!)

Next, we find Bogart as company manager on tours of Brady productions, work which also entailed understudying the male parts and playing minor roles. One such part was that of a Japanese houseboy who walked on stage with a tray of cocktails and uttered a single line (or perhaps two; and did he or did he not drop the tray?).

At any rate Bogart progressed to the juvenile lead in a play called *Swifty*. (He was to become dreadfully familiar with juvenile leads and defined them as characters who kept the play going while the principals nipped off stage to change their costumes.) The young actor was promptly impaled on the vitriolic pen of critic Alexander Woollcott who described his performance in the comedy (which lasted a mere week) as 'What is usually and mercifully described as inadequate'. Bogart loved to quote this barb when subsequent success had fully anaesthetized the pain.

Other parts followed, mostly in light romantic comedies, though *Nerves* was a war drama that was produced by his friend, Bill Brady Jr, and flopped. His hits included *Meet the Wife* (1923), playing a newspaperman with Mary Boland and

Bogart as a handsome and earnest juvenile actor on Broadway

Clifton Webb; *Hell's Bells* (1925), playing a dandy opposite Shirley Booth; and *Cradle Snatchers* (1925), opposite Mary Boland and Edna May Oliver. The latter play gave Bogart much satisfaction when a prominent critic, Amy Leslie, reviewed the Chicago try-out and declared that Bogart was 'as young and handsome as Valentino, as dexterous and elegant in comedy as E. H. Sothern, as graceful as any of our best romantic actors'. That clipping went into his wallet next to the Woollcott blast, to which it provided the ideal antidote.

On 20 May 1926, Bogart married the prominent stage actress Helen Menken. His career soon nosedived: he appeared with Roscoe 'Fatty' Arbuckle, who was making a doomed attempt to retrieve his pre-scandal popularity by performing in the comedy *Baby Mine*, which collapsed after twelve performances. Bogart went after work in Chicago; Helen took off for a good job in London. Conflicting career demands soon broke up their marriage.

A leading role in the light comedy *Saturday's Children* kept Bogart busy for a good part of 1927, but when the hit came to be filmed as a part talkie no thought was apparently given to using an actor whose performance had been, according to one critic, 'full of charm and humour'.

In 1928 Bogart renewed an acquaintance with actress Mary Phillips, who had appeared with him in *Nerves*. She became his second wife that year; they remained married until 1937 (she kept up her stage career). During the late twenties, Bogart kept busy in a mixture of summer stock, quick flops and solid successes on Broadway. He survived the great stock market crash of October 1929 in a hit play called *It's a Wise Child*. During its run, the movies beckoned.

4. TO HOLLYWOOD & BACK

W arner Bros. were then busy making a series of talking shorts mostly of a musical variety, through a subsidiary, The Vitaphone Corporation, at a studio in Brooklyn. A good many featured singer Ruth Etting, and for at least one of these, *Broadway's Like That*, Humphrey Bogart was cast – apparently as a man about town taking advantage of a girl from the sticks. Meanwhile Fox, along with the other Hollywood studios, was constantly on the look-out for well-spoken Broadway players who might fit into the new era of all-talking pictures. With a brother-in-law working in Fox's New York office, Bogart was soon screen-tested. The results were encouraging enough to put him on the westbound train with the promise of starring in a re-make of the 1924 hit, *The Man Who Came Back*. But the same carrot had been dangled in front of other hopefuls from the East and the role was eventually assigned to an established movie star, Charles Farrell, with Bogart given the consolatory position of voice coach on the production.

However, Fox were clearly serious about using Humphrey Bogart and gave him good roles in two of their big 1930 releases. Since he had made his reputation in light comedy, it is no surprise to discover that he was handed parts in like vein.

Up the River (1930) gave Bogart the chance to work with John Ford, even then a front-rank director, though he reputedly made a poor impression on Ford by being too familiar and was never to work with the director again. Another young Fox hopeful of that time, John Wayne, had a more respectful friendship with Ford that was directly responsible for his eventual stardom in *Stagecoach*.

A broad comedy, *Up the River* was about a couple of tough convicts, St. Louis (Spencer Tracy, another stage recruit making his screen debut) and his thickheaded pal, Dannemora Dan (Warren Hymer). The pair befriend Bogart, who is serving time for 'accidental manslaughter'. Bogart falls in love with a girl in the women's wing who was the dupe of a swindler. When he gets out and returns home to his parents (who think he's been abroad), a blackmailer threatens to expose his past. The two convicts escape from jail and sort out his troubles, enabling him to marry the girl (Claire Luce) and live happily ever after. Then the pair return to prison for an important baseball game. The story has striking parallels with one of Bogart's favourite later films, *We're No Angels* (1955). 'Efficient' was the word the *New York Times* attached to Bogart's work in *Up the River*.

According to William K. Everson, who has viewed the one badly damaged known surviving print, 'Bogart is amusingly subdued in the scenes where, as an ex-convict now living with a mother unaware of his past, he dutifully calls "Coming, mother!" and trots downstairs like a slightly cynical Henry Aldrich!'

Up the River (1930): Bogart and Claire Luce handled the romance in this broad comedy directed by John Ford

Overleaf: In *A Devil with Women* (1930), Bogart fights bandits in a banana republic, supported by Mona Maris and (inset) gets tough with Michael Vavitch as the leader of the revolutionaries

A Devil with Women (1930) partnered him with burly Victor McLaglen, who had a role little removed from his famous Captain Flagg characterization – a mercenary seeking to capture a revolutionary in a banana republic. Bogart was a sort of junior Quirt as Tom Standish, McLaglen's ally and romantic rival who is eventually successful in both winning the girl (Mona Maris) and keeping the older man's friendship. Said Mordaunt Hall in the *New York Times*: '. . . there is an irritating friend with his trick of getting the last laugh, whether it be at martial or at amorous adventure. The last is Humphrey Bogart who . . . gives an ingratiating performance. Mr. Bogart is both good looking and intelligent.' But to at least one historian, Bogart now seems distinctly 'uncomfortable'.

Suddenly Fox seemed to lose interest in him. In *Body and Soul* (1931) he portrayed an American flyer in an R.A.F. squadron in France during World War I. He has become involved with a girl in England although he has an American wife. He dies trying to bring down a German observation balloon, leaving his pal (played by Charles Farrell) to complete the job and award him credit posthumously. Most of the picture detailed Farrell's adventures with Bogart's widow and his English girlfriend, one of whom turns out to be a German spy. Though Bogart dominated the early scenes, it must have been galling for him to relinquish the meatier part of the film to Charles Farrell.

Bogart, as a flyer in wartorn France, only lasted for a couple of reels of *Body and Soul* (1931). Charles Farrell (centre) headed the cast; Donald Dillaway is seen at left

Fox then dispatched him to Universal for *Bad Sister* (1931).
He played a heel called Valentine Corliss who romances the
daughter (Sidney Fox) of a wealthy businessman and uses her
to extract money from wealthy townspeople for a mythical
factory scheme. He decamps with the girl, abandoning her at
the first opportunity, leaving her to return home sadder and
wiser. As the foolish girl's younger sister, Bette Davis made
her screen debut. Carl Laemmle Jr, the new head of production at Universal, is said to have advised both Davis and Bogart
that they didn't photograph well and should hasten back to the
stage. A recent revival of the picture shows Bogart giving an
assured performance but Davis failing lamentably.

Bogart must have known he wasn't going to make it at Fox
when he reported for *Women of All Nations* (1931). He was no
longer sharing the action with star Victor McLaglen as he had
in *A Devil with Women* but was one of the supporters, a marine
called Stone, in this second sequel to *What Price Glory?* Even
more humiliating than coming ninth in the cast was his total
absence from the film in its final form! A recently revived print,
at the full (though rather brief) running time, shows no sign of
him and several other billed players.

Fox rubbed in Bogart's downfall by giving him a role in a
George O'Brien western, *A Holy Terror* (1931). It was a sad
fate for a stage actor – not only to be playing in a 53-minute

29

cowboy programmer but being padded out and fitted with elevator shoes to make a more manly impression! The part was that of ranch foreman Steve Nash and required him to sulk when a dashing millionaire (O'Brien) flies in from the East and takes away his girl (Sally Eilers). Being neither hero nor villain, he was essentially just running errands and helping to fill in the background.

He was then supposed to go into a Spencer Tracy drama at Fox called *She Wanted a Millionaire* (1932) but didn't, unless his part was too small to be credited. He quit the studio and retraced his steps to Broadway.

His first play there, John van Druten's *After All*, quickly died and Bogart was relieved to be summoned back to Holly-wood by Harry Cohn, boss of Columbia Pictures, for the top male role in *Love Affair* (1932). The film was essentially a

In *Big City Blues* (1932) Bogart and Lyle Talbot quarrel over Josephine Dunn at a party

Three on a Match (1932):
Bogart and Lyle Talbot
quarrelling again, with Ann
Dvorak as the haggard
mother held captive with
her child. Her pleas to
Bogart, in his first role as a
gun-toting heavy, to show
compassion cut no ice

vehicle for an English actress, Dorothy Mackaill, a silent star trying to hang on in talkies; Columbia was not then a major studio. It made a habit of picking up other studio's discards: John Wayne also went there after Fox was through with him. But the part was a meaty one. Mackaill is an heiress; Bogart is Jim Leonard, an engineer trying to promote a new aircraft engine. They have an affair but she leaves him rather than distract him from his work. She even agrees to marry another suitor in order to finance Bogart's engine. Following various plot complications, she is only saved from committing suicide by the last minute arrival of Bogart. The part did not revitalize the actor's screen career but he struck up a friendship with Harry Cohn, revived years later at Columbia.

Bogart is usually associated with Warner Bros. in film histories – and rightly so, for he made far more pictures there than anywhere else. His very first work for Warners was in 1932: a couple of roles that were little more than bits.

Big City Blues is a minor comedy-drama about a callow youth from Indiana (Eric Linden) who spends three hectic days in the big city of New York being fleeced by a cousin and suspected of murder. Bogart appears as Shep Adkins – by profession an assistant theatre treasurer – who is a member of the drinking party that assembles in the boy's hotel room. He quarrels over a woman with another guest (Lyle Talbot) and they start to fight, making use of broken bottles. The fight spreads, the room is plunged into darkness, and a girl is murdered. . . . It is interesting to watch Bogart getting the feel of a touchy, truculent figure: the familiar traits are there, a little stiff and subdued. The part is strictly one-dimensional but Bogart gives it substance.

In *Three on a Match* (1932), Bogart makes his first screen appearance as a tough hoodlum or 'mug' called Harve. He leads a gang who work for a big-time gambler (Edward Arnold). Lyle Talbot plays another gambler in debt to Arnold. When Talbot kidnaps the wife (Ann Dvorak) and son of a wealthy lawyer (Warren William), Bogart and his boys butt in to make sure the ransom is properly collected. Bogart did his best but the part had too little variation and insufficient screen time to indicate that he would ever make a notable new screen villain.

Once again he went back to Broadway where he was better appreciated. But the going was tough even there; as the Depression bit harder, spending money dried up, and few plays lasted a month. Bogart got what work he could and was pleased to hear from a successful stage producer, Chester Erskine, who told me recently: 'We lived near each other at that time in New York. Bogart was a very good actor and still playing juveniles – as he used to describe them, the "Tennis, anyone?" roles. I said, "I'm going to make a film. There's a part in it for you but it's a heavy, a tough guy." And he said, "Well, I can do that!" And he did it – very well. He was intrigued by the thought that he was breaking with his past, he loved the idea of playing a part in which he was not sympathetic. Only a year or so later, he said, "I've talked them into letting me play *The Petrified Forest*," and that was that, he was really off!'

Erskine's film was called *Midnight* (1934) and he re-opened the old Thomas Edison studios to shoot it for less than $50,000. Bogart had poor billing – eighth place – as a gangster called Garboni. The film was an ironical melodrama. A jury foreman (O. P. Heggie) has been instrumental in dispatching a woman to the electric chair for a crime of passion; at the same instant as the switch is pulled, history repeats itself and his daughter (Sidney Fox) shoots her deceitful racketeer lover (Bogart, of course) in circumstances paralleling the earlier crime.

A studio portrait of Humphrey Bogart

5. ENTER
DUKE MANTEE

Bogart polished his command of villainy in a short-lived play called *Invitation to Murder* and was observed by producer Arthur Hopkins, in the throes of casting *The Petrified Forest*. It seems to have been Bogart's voice that suggested him for the role of Duke Mantee, an escaped killer modelled on Dillinger, but the playwright, Robert Sherwood, saw Bogart as the footballer, his play's nearest equivalent to a 'Tennis, anyone?' part. Hopkins arranged for Bogart to audition for Mantee and the play's star, English actor Leslie Howard, had only to hear Bogart to insist on having him. The play opened in Boston on Christmas Eve, 1934 to acclaim, and premiered in New York on 7 January 1935, settling down for a run of 194 performances. It was a really Happy New Year for Bogart.

The film rights were snapped up by Warner Bros. who were more than pleased to have Leslie Howard in the film version. But they didn't want a Hollywood has-been to play Duke Mantee, and certainly not when they had Edward G. Robinson on hand. Fortunately, Robinson was tired of gangster parts and turned this one down while an alarmed Bogart rallied Leslie Howard to his cause. Howard obliged by quietly insisting that he would play with no one but Humphrey Bogart.

The rest is history. Bogart succeeded this time round in Hollywood. He knew his Duke Mantee inside out by now and the nearly foolproof part had a saturnine quality that suited his personality better than the flippancy of lighter roles.

Seen today, *The Petrified Forest* (1936) is something of a creaking curiosity, especially during the Bogartless opening half hour. The setting – a remote service-station and café in the rugged Arizona desert – is impressively but obviously created on the Warner sound stages, lending a useful 'closed in' feeling to the film. A friendship blossoms between two sensitive, lonely people: a penniless British wanderer (Leslie Howard) who is seeking to put some meaning back into his life and a French-born waitress (Bette Davis) who yearns to escape from her deadening surroundings. Then Humphrey Bogart's Duke Mantee, a killer who (radio broadcasts tell us) has left eight men dead in a shootout in Oklahoma City turns up with his gang. He takes over the place, and awaits the arrival of his girlfriend.

Bogart's performance is powerful – and primitive. He shuffles round the café setting, hands hanging limply in front of him, head drooping forward, sinking into his shoulders, making it only too clear that he is one of the 'apes' with whom Leslie Howard earlier contrasted intellectuals like himself, in talking to the waitress about the future of mankind. Bogart speaks his lines wearily and heavily; his slow, clear enunciation would seem to be a leftover from his stage experience in the role. His Mantee is in sharp contrast to the aggressive, volatile, optimistic public enemies of earlier Hollywood films.

This famous publicity pose for *The Petrified Forest* (1936) shows Leslie Howard and Bette Davis as the brave lovers, with Bogart as the escaped killer Duke Mantee who apparently threatens their happiness. The desert backdrop is as unconvincing here as it was in the film

35

'This is Duke Mantee, the world-famous killer, and he's hungry,' says one of his gang as he first enters, immediately reducing the figure of legend to a man who needs to eat like the rest of us. 'You're the last great apostle of rugged individualism,' declares Leslie Howard, raising his glass in salute to Bogart who has settled down, shotgun resting on his lap, on a platform a step above his prisoners like a king on a throne. Bogart spits out the end he has bitten off a cigar and responds to Howard's tribute – 'Maybe you're right, pal' – his answer indicating his ignorance of what Howard means. 'He ain't no gangster, he's a real old-time desperado. Gangsters is foreigners,' Charley Grapewin's Gramps tells us, but when Leslie Howard invites Bogart to build up his legend by describing his colourful life, the outlaw gives a tired reply: 'Wha' d'you tink? I spend most of my time since I grew up in jail. And it looks like I spend the rest of my life dead.'

Howard is concerned to ennoble Bogart as a suitable instrument for his own demise, for he arranges with him to be shot dead so that the waitress can receive enough money from his life insurance policy to escape to France. She represents hope for the future in a film where the conventional hero figure – the burly football player – is ridiculed for his shallowness and philistinism. Howard recognizes that both he and Bogart have had their day. But Bogart becomes a figure of pathos as he fails to measure up to Howard's valuation of him. Though he agrees to Howard's request to be killed, he refuses to carry it out when the time comes until it is a matter of his own immediate survival when Howard blocks his escape route. And he proves to be no great man of incisive action when the pressure is on. 'Shut up! Give me time to think!' Bogart cries as he learns his girl has betrayed their whereabouts and his men exhort him to flee. As he steps past the dying Howard, he

Bullets or Ballots (1936): the climactic confrontation between Bogart and Edward G. Robinson, the latter playing an ex-cop who has been betraying Bogart's crime organization

stops to say, 'Be seeing you soon.' Moments later his capture by the police is relayed to us.

Fortunately for Bogart, playwright Robert Sherwood's attempts to write an epitaph for the American gangster were unsuccessful, and the actor embarked on a hectic schedule, largely playing villains, for his next few years as a Warners contract artist.

His very next role was that of a gangster, this time of the urban variety, clean-shaven and smartly dressed, in *Bullets or Ballots* (1936). As Nick 'Bugs' Fenner, he added up to quite a lethal figure, responsible during the film for knocking off his crime czar boss, a crusading newspaper editor, *and* the cop who worms his way into the organization. Bogart himself proved to be quite a dangerous scene stealer, especially where Barton MacLane is concerned. At the start of the film, he takes MacLane (as his boss, Al Kruger) to a movie theatre to see a crime documentary in which MacLane is denounced as a public enemy. While MacLane turns his back to buy tickets, Bogart moves around in his best alert bodyguard manner. Inside, while MacLane sits there stolidly gazing at the screen, Bogart tugs thoughtfully at his lip and later fingers it again; he shakes his head slightly with amusement at what's on the screen; and he glances at MacLane to see his reaction. All this ensures that one watches Bogart rather than MacLane, who was always a dull if competent performer. Bogart even contrives to gain a lighting advantage in a later scene in MacLane's office, standing over a desk lamp that gives a sinister cast to his features while MacLane sits behind the desk, neutrally lit. MacLane is billed above Bogart here, but it is easy to see why MacLane slipped to smaller parts and Bogart went on to bigger things.

Bogart's part is the livelier one, anyway, as the figure who stirs up trouble while MacLane tries to keep things quiet and peaceful: Bogart shoots down Henry O'Neill's newsman on his own initiative and later he appears in MacLane's office in a slightly low-angle, menacing shot to announce that he's taking over and fires his gun to prove the point.

Bogart's main adversary is Edward G. Robinson, the cop who once put him in hospital for a week, and who now is a trusted member of the crime organization. When Bogart has proof that Robinson is an undercover agent, he rushes to the man's boarding house and catches him coming down the stairs. They draw their guns and blaze away. Though Bogart must die and Robinson survive long enough to incriminate the bankers who are behind the organization, Bogart finds a way to fix his death in the audience's mind: as Edward G. Robinson steps over his corpse, his hand is lodged against a stair, frozen in a farewell wave.

Bogart next had his first experience of the Bryan Foy unit at Warner Bros. which specialized in cheap re-makes of the studio's old hits. He was given Edward G. Robinson's role in *Five Star Final* (1931). The new version was called *Two Against the World* (1936) and switched the earlier film's powerful attack on yellow journalism to a radio station setting. Bogart is station manager Sherry Scott; he reluctantly accepts his boss's scheme to revive a twenty-year-old scandal, resigns after the broadcast has tragic repercussions and helps the Radio Commission clean up the station's policies. Bogart could not give his part the maturity that Edward G. Robinson had invested in the original.

China Clipper (1936) was excitingly topical at the time: it now seems an overweight, undistinguished drama. Pat O'Brien bulldozes a new plane off the drawing board into the air for a record-breaking run across the Pacific. Bogart and Ross Alexander are his pilot buddies. Alexander was personable, and so had the humour and romance; they made Bogart a widower and more sombre. He tears a strip off O'Brien for his callous methods of driving his men, knocking him to the ground and leaving; but he returns in time, as if you ever doubted it, to pilot the historical flight. The emphasis, though, is less on his contribution than on montaged newspaper headlines and O'Brien sweating it out by the wireless on the ground.

Isle of Fury (1936) gave Bogart the leading role but was another of Bryan Foy's rehashes, this time of *The Narrow Corner* (1933). The resulting picture threw out the subtleties of the original but clung on to all the plot complications. Bogart's Val Stevens (he grew a moustache for the part) is a wanted man hiding out on a South Seas island; he so impresses Donald Woods, the detective on his trail, that the latter leaves him to enjoy married life with his bride (Margaret Lindsay).

Black Legion, the first of seven films in which Bogart was seen during 1937, was altogether superior. An example of Warner Bros. in its crusading mood, it cast Bogart as an ordinary factory worker who joins a xenophobic organization, the Black Legion, to compensate for the frustration he experiences at work when a studious Pole (Henry Brandon) gains the promotion that he covets.

Bogart's Frank Taylor starts out as a likeable family man, proud of his wife and child and planning to improve their lives with the extra income he expects to receive. His reaction to hearing of butter on the table – 'What is this? Christmas or something?' – brings home the real deprivation of the period and the frustration it bred.

Sore at losing the promotion, Bogart is susceptible to talk of 'the foreign menace' and 'America for Americans'. It is specific circumstances rather than his natural disposition that makes him ripe for membership of the Black Legion: he joins a little hesitantly and balks at the theatrical language of the pledge of allegiance he has to read during the initiation cere-

Black Legion (1937): Bogart, recruited into a terror organization, reluctantly accepts a gun which he can ill afford to pay for

mony. But, once in, his subsequent disintegration is rapid. He admires himself in a full-length mirror, tucking a gun into his belt; he gets his revenge on the Pole; he wrecks his marriage, loses his job, and ends up killing his best friend (Dick Foran) after drunkenly confiding his membership of the terror organization. In court, the old Frank Taylor asserts himself, easing his conscience by a full confession.

Regrettably, the film is too schematic and prodding, harping on Bogart's impending promotion to the point that one knows he isn't going to get it. And the film betrays itself by representing the Black Legion as the creation of businessmen whose motive is not hatred of foreigners but the lucrative income from selling guns and cloaks! But Bogart confidently handles a wide range of moods: heady optimism, sullen resentment, drunken self-pity, conscience-striken remorse. He only overplays the scene where he begs Foran not to turn him in after he has blurted out his secret: Bogart could never humble himself convincingly. At the climax, he is deemed too inarticulate a character actually to denounce the Black Legion and the job is turned over to the ever-eloquent Samuel S. Hinds as the judge, leaving Bogart with only a last distressed look to cast in his wife's direction as he is led away to the cells. Undoubtedly Warners could afford to cast Bogart in such a big role because the subject was the film's main selling point.

The studio's evaluation of his drawing power was indicated by another role (like that of *China Clipper*) in support of Pat O'Brien. *The Great O'Malley*, a thick slice of Irish whimsy, had Bogart cast as John Phillips, the unemployed family man who is going after a good job when an officious cop, O'Malley (Pat O'Brien), stops his car and fines him for having a noisy silencer. Losing the job, the embittered Bogart turns to a life of crime and is arrested for a pawnshop hold-up when the same O'Malley delays his getaway by catching him with that car silencer still not mended. The cop befriends Bogart's crippled daughter, arranges for an operation on her leg, and wins a parole for Bogart. Unaware that his old enemy has become his benefactor, Bogart shoots him at the first opportunity but the understanding cop passes it off as an accident and everything ends happily ever after.

Marked Woman was altogether sterner stuff. Like *Black Legion*, it was derived from actual events. For a change Bogart played an uncomplicated, incorrigibly honest figure, an assistant District Attorney called David Graham who is itching to nail vice czar Johnny Vanning (Eduardo Ciannelli). Bogart's character was modelled on Thomas A. Dewey, who had smashed the prostitution racket of Charles 'Lucky' Luciano. Bogart's eagerness to trap his man leads him into trusting Bette Davis's clip-joint hostess (the word 'prostitute' was not permissible) but her evidence is discredited by other witnesses as she well knew it would be. 'So long, chump! I'll be seeing

Overleaf:
Above left: In *Kid Galahad* (1937) Bogart was supremely nasty as a fights racketeer, here seen humiliating the bellhop, played by Wayne Morris. Bette Davis and Edward G. Robinson are the nearest observers; Harry Carey, Sr and Ben Welden are in the background behind Bette Davis

Above right: Bogart played the honest prosecutor seeking to smash a vice racket in *Marked Woman* (1937). Bette Davis was one of the 'hostesses' employed at a clip-joint

Below: *San Quentin* (1937) Bogart is not amused to learn from a fellow prisoner (Ernie Adams) that his sister is dating one of the prison officers. Bogart's pal (Joe Sawyer) lends a restraining hand

you,' she calls as she breezes out of court past Bogart. Later, however, Davis's younger sister (Jane Bryan) becomes entangled with Ciannelli and meets with a fatal accident at his hands. Bogart at first seems to delight in Davis's distress but once the sister's body is found, and she has been scarred by Ciannelli's men to keep her quiet, he knows he can trust her, brings a case against Ciannelli, and clinches matters with a long, hard-hitting address to the jury. Bogart reputedly overheard technicians betting on how many takes he would need to get the speech right; he wagered he could do it first time, and did.

Paradoxically, the film's most telling scene was not the conviction of Ciannelli but the aftermath in which Bogart reaps all the acclaim (and is even hailed as the state's future governor) at the expense of Davis and the other girls who have made his success possible with their courageous evidence. Bogart admirably captures the awkwardness of the man as he tries to express his admiration, concern, indebtedness and, maybe, affection for Bette Davis but can only utter the lame promise, 'No matter what you do or where you go, we'll meet again.' 'Goodbye, then, I'll be seeing you,' says Davis wistfully, in complete contrast to her earlier brash farewell, using the same words, after she let Bogart down in court. They go their separate ways: he back to the flashlights of the press photographers, she into the night with the other girls. One of them was played by Mayo Methot, whom Bogart eventually made his

third wife on 20 August 1938. Their stormy relationship (they were known as 'The Battling Bogarts') lasted until 1945.

Despite sparse screen time in *Kid Galahad*, Bogart contrived – on his first collaboration with director Michael Curtiz – to make a striking impression as a thoroughly nasty and humourless piece of work, a fights racketeer called Turkey Morgan. He is memorably introduced walking in on a boisterous three-day party with a bunch of his mugs and chilling the room to silence. When he proceeds to humiliate a bellhop by shortening his trouser legs with a flick-knife, no one dares intervene. It is this same bellhop (played by Wayne Morris) that the honest fights promoter Nick Donati (Edward G. Robinson) grooms into a contender for the heavyweight title held by Bogart's man. When Robinson, for reasons of spite, arranges with Bogart for his fighter to lose the match, then changes his mind and helps him win, Bogart goes down to the dressing rooms to have his revenge.

Here Curtiz inserts his familiar directorial signature of shadows on a wall to show Bogart firing his gun to draw off the police and reporters who are thronging the new champ's dressing rooms so that he can reach Robinson. Only when Robinson casually asks about the commotion do we learn just how gratuitously callous Bogart is. His shot has struck a spectator, 'an insurance salesman from out of town – first time here'. The information about the victim is just specific enough to evoke some sympathy and thoroughly condemn Bogart. When Robinson enters his washroom, Bogart is waiting behind the door. Bogart even manages to kill Robinson in the shootout that follows but is fatally wounded himself and makes the simple matter of dropping dead an attention-seizing affair as he flops with an arm across his chest, wrist curled after dropping his weapon. Robinson dies more slowly, having a death-bed speech to deliver.

By playing Turkey within a very narrow range centring on a surly malevolence, Bogart sacrificed colour and variety in favour of an intensity reinforced by the actor's splendid command of mean glares and lip-curling snarls; his stiffness of manner appropriately suggested a lack of flexibility. In a part like this, there was absolutely nothing to suggest that Bogart had any prospect of becoming a romantic leading man!

San Quentin was Bogart's first dramatic prison story, a high-speed affair in which he capably played the role of a man far younger than himself. He was a cocky 25-year-old, Red Kennedy, going inside for the first time after a career of five years in reform school and a year in the county jail that has left him with an ingrained anti-social attitude. As he proudly boasts, 'I kicked a guy in the face once because he was a cop.'

In the prison yard, he's the one with the brim of his regulation hat turned furthest back as a gesture of defiance. Later, he wavers between the good influence of the fair-minded new captain of the prison yard (Pat O'Brien) and the bad influence of a confirmed criminal (Joe Sawyer). When Bogart learns that his precious sister (Ann Sheridan) is dating the captain, he explodes with rage, broods in his bunk, then stages an escape while on the road gang. He shoots O'Brien before discovering that his sister and O'Brien love each other. In a brave attempt to make amends, Bogart starts back to the prison, is fired on by the police, and staggers along in a skilfully prolonged collapse that owes more to ballet than drama. He dies in the shadow of the prison gates exhorting his fellow cons to back up their yard captain. *San Quentin* is still fun, an absolutely archetypal prison movie with no delusions of social significance.

Like *The Petrified Forest*, Samuel Goldwyn's *Dead End* was a film version of a Broadway play that thoughtfully probed the impact of the gangster on American life. Since Bogart had proved, in playing Duke Mantee, that he knew how to handle a serious gangster figure, he was an obvious candidate for the role of Baby Face Martin in *Dead End* and was borrowed from Warners to work for director William Wyler.

Above: In *Dead End* (1937) Bogart and his pal (Allen Jenkins) lurk in the shadows where they belong while strapping hero Joel McCrea gives vent to his hatred of all that Bogart represents

Bogart's Martin is thirty-one years old with eight murders behind him; he pays a nostalgic visit to the slum street where he was born, protected from recognition by plastic surgery. Bogart is toying with the idea of settling down with his girlfriend of ten years before. He discovers that she has become a prostitute. He also expects a warm welcome from his mother (Marjorie Main), who promptly slaps his face and denounces him, snarling 'You dog, you dirty yellow dog, you! You ain't no son of mine!' 'I killed a guy for looking at me the way you are now!' Bogart hisses back at his mother. His subsequent reasoning is sharp and to the point: 'I came home for something. I didn't get it. I'm coming out with something – even if it's only dough.'

So Bogart recruits some of the slum kids to help him kidnap a rich youth. He incurs the wrath of Joel McCrea who has spent six years studying to become an architect and represents the best kind of slum product, just as Bogart represents the worst. They are natural adversaries and when McCrea actually kills Bogart in hand-to-hand combat it is a symbolic victory of the builder over the destroyer. McCrea's success also earns him a huge reward to ensure a bright future.

Bogart's Martin is a memorably ugly and touchy figure, more insidiously evil than most of the Hollywood gangsters of the thirties, proud of his achievements but at the same time aware that he has reached a dead end both literally (the dead end street of the title) and figuratively, as his sentimental hopes for the future are dashed.

Still on loan from Warners, Bogart was reunited with Leslie Howard for a mild comedy about Hollywood called *Stand-In*, the last of the films he was seen in during 1937. Based, like *Mr. Deeds Goes to Town*, on a story by Clarence Budington Kel-

land, it told a similar story of a young innocent plunged into a strange and somewhat hostile environment and finding his feet with the help of a girl. Here it was Leslie Howard as the New York accountant investigating the plight of a movie studio with the help of the stand-in played by Joan Blondell. Bogart was Douglas Quintain, the studio production chief who has taken to the bottle since breaking up with the studio's biggest star, Cheri (Marla Shelton). While Howard unearths a scheme involving Cheri and the studio's prize director, Koslofski (Alan Mowbray), to sabotage the studio and lower its selling price, Bogart provides the cutting room skill to turn their feeble adventure picture into a hilarious comedy that will save the company. Bogart seemed to spend most of the time standing around holding a black Scottie; he had little chance to register, though he does obtain a strong laugh from the glance of sour disgust he gives Alan Mowbray after they have just had a private screening of his dreadful picture.

The kind of roles that awaited Bogart on his return to the Warner lot suggest that he was in temporary disgrace, perhaps after feuding with Jack Warner. Bogart regarded *Swing Your Lady* (1938) as his worst film, and it probably was. It certainly wasted him as a wrestling promoter, down on his luck and stranded in the wilds of Missouri, who comes up with the harebrained idea of pitting his wrestler (Nat Pendleton) against a powerful woman blacksmith (Louize Fazenda). The result was hillbilly farce.

Crime School (1938) was better – and what's more, an unexpected box-office smash hit. It put Bogart back with the Dead End Kids who had been the delinquents he tried to corrupt in the Goldwyn picture. The film was mostly a re-make of James Cagney's 1933 *The Mayor of Hell* but it revived the romantic misunderstanding of *San Quentin* – Bryan Foy wasn't missing any chances. When Cagney had played it, he was a brash young hoodlum who gets a political appointment of running a reformatory and wins the kids over by talking to them on their own level. Bogart wasn't youthful enough for that approach, and played a social worker who was running the reformatory on progressive lines, much to the disgust of the tyrannical superintendent (Cy Kendall) who gets his own back by making a young inmate believe Bogart is misbehaving with his sister. He and some friends break out and go after Bogart with a gun. Bogart offered steady sincerity in the role and *Crime School* is one of his more rewarding pictures of this period.

Men Are Such Fools (1938), however, is best avoided like the plague. A 'sophisticated' comedy set in the advertising world with Bogart as an agency executive, it introduces him, after some twenty minutes, having a poolside chitchat with heroine Priscilla Lane. He falls for her and keeps her late at the office when she should be home with her husband (Wayne Morris).

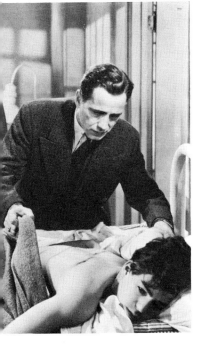

Below: As a social worker in *Crime School* (1938), Bogart is horrified to find evidence of brutality on the body of Billy Halop, playing a boy at reform school

'I'm probably a cad,' Bogart declares. 'Are you by any chance a weak woman? Oh, too bad. In that case I'll have to be a strong cad.' As if such scintillating dialogue wasn't bad enough, Bogart undergoes the further insult of being knocked to the ground by an irate Wayne Morris and just staying there.

Here is as good a place as any to emphasize that Bogart was a totally professional actor. Even when the parts were as insultingly trivial as this, he played them straight and to the best of his ability, when it would have been perfectly understandable for him to have hammed them up or said his lines half-heartedly.

In *The Amazing Dr Clitterhouse* (1938) Bogart's screen image was amusingly sent up as criminologist Edward G. Robinson describes him as 'a magnificent specimen of pure viciousness.' Bogart does his best to live up to this estimate when Robinson, to further his research into the criminal temperament, displaces him as the leader of a gang of thieves. Eventually he drives Robinson into extending his experiments to murder, and the essentially comic tone of the film evaporates as Bogart, having downed a poisoned drink, struggles to remain conscious and Robinson keenly records the details of his slow collapse, then despatches him to be dumped in the river. The film's splendid ending has Robinson brought to trial for Bogart's murder, persuading a jury by his claim to perfect sanity that the opposite must be the case, and being acquitted!

Racket Busters (1938) was the kind of brisk, minor drama on which Bogart received top billing. Here was another of his misanthropic villains, looking out over New York city by night, flashing his teeth in a mirthless smile, and crying 'Hello, suckers!' He sets his gang to work muscling in on the fruit and produce market, then makes brief appearances from time to time, probably when he could be spared from some other film he was making simultaneously. George Brent played the trucker who eventually turns against Bogart's organization and chases him down an alleyway for the ritual private showdown between hero and villain. Bogart now pays the price of having left the dirty work to his men: when he tries to gun down Brent, he shows himself to be an appallingly bad shot. He fires twice at close range missing both times, putting one bullet in the floor beside Brent's foot. The obligatory final scene showed Bogart, sulking and unrepentant, listening to the judge (Charles Trowbridge) denounce him as an enemy of society.

Angels with Dirty Faces (1938) was a big picture – which, at this stage of Bogart's career, meant that his role had to be minor. He was at his most slippery and shifty as a lawyer who welshes on a deal to pay James Cagney for taking a three year sentence for a crime they both committed. Cagney claims what's his at gunpoint and also takes some incriminating

Centre: Humphrey Bogart as a double-crossing lawyer reluctantly makes a phone call in *Angels with Dirty Faces* (1938)

Right: death comes in the same film—in the violent fashion to which Bogart was then well accustomed

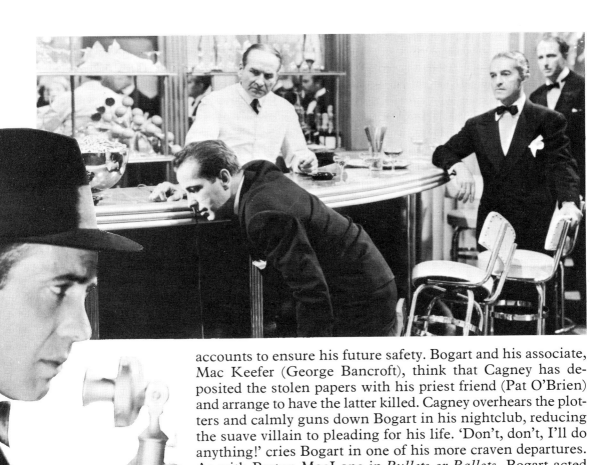

accounts to ensure his future safety. Bogart and his associate, Mac Keefer (George Bancroft), think that Cagney has deposited the stolen papers with his priest friend (Pat O'Brien) and arrange to have the latter killed. Cagney overhears the plotters and calmly guns down Bogart in his nightclub, reducing the suave villain to pleading for his life. 'Don't, don't, I'll do anything!' cries Bogart in one of his more craven departures. As with Barton MacLane in *Bullets or Ballots*, Bogart acted rings around George Bancroft whose elementary style left him with only physical size to his advantage.

1939 was another busy and rather undistinguished year for Bogart. He was seen in six films. In *King of the Underworld* Bryan Foy devised a way of re-making *Doctor Socrates* (1935) by giving Kay Francis the Paul Muni role (!) of a doctor who outwits a gang of crooks. Bogart gained the part of the ruthless gang leader that Barton MacLane had undertaken. His Joe Gurney had some entertaining aspects: he captures a writer and commissions a biography that will do justice to his vision of himself as a latter-day Napoleon (that idea came from Warners' 1930 gangster film, *Doorway to Hell*). Bogart's downfall arrives when Kay Francis contrives to temporarily blind him with an eyedrop solution and the police shoot him on a first floor landing. He tumbles down the stairs, clutches his bleeding chest, and makes a last request that no one should know the new Napoleon was outwitted by a woman.

In *The Oklahoma Kid*, Cagney and Bogart played contrasting species of Western badmen. Cagney was the Kid, a colourful rascal and a good guy at heart. Bogart was Whip McCord, garbed in black from head to foot, the crooked boss of Tulsa City with only curled hair alleviating his grim appearance.

45

Bogart doesn't really have much to do, but from the introductory shot of him nodding his head thoughtfully as he watches a consignment of gold being unloaded from a train, he brings a powerful presence to the role.

His first run-in with Cagney is entertaining. He steps forward, puffing out his chest. 'My name's Whip McCord. Does that mean anything to you?' Cagney thinks a moment, then comments, 'I don't like it,' before turning to the man next to him to ask, 'Do you?'

After Bogart has incited a mob to lynch Cagney's law-abiding father, Cagney slips into the back of Bogart's saloon to settle the score. Arriving on the first floor landing, he has a chair bounced off the back of his head by the waiting Bogart. They exchange a few blows and carry the fight downstairs by crashing through the bannisters in the traditional way. After some more action with chairs and broken bottles, Bogart attempts to gun down his opponent and is shot dead. The film is a brisk affair with Bogart once again the perfect tinder for Cagney's explosive temperament.

You Can't Get Away with Murder is routine but undeniably entertaining. Bogart is Frank Wilson, a petty crook who kills a pawnbroker in a hold-up and is scared his young accomplice (Billy Halop, one of the Dead End Kids) will give him away. They are both put in jail on another charge, and then the youngster starts to weaken. Bogart takes the boy with him on a jailbreak and shoots him, hoping to pass off the wounds as the result of police fire before he surrendered. But the youngster lives long enough to put Bogart in the electric chair.

Edmund Goulding's classic 'weepie', *Dark Victory*, favourite film of its star Bette Davis, is a rare instance of Bogart's presence not enhancing a picture. Woefully miscast as a brash, cheerful Irish groom, Michael O'Leary (a lock of hair curled forward on to his forehead to make him seem young enough for the part), he made a brave attempt to don an appropriate accent and give a lilting rhythm to his speech – but to no avail.

Fortunately, the part was not a sizeable one, providing him with only one major scene. In that he pours out his frustrations to Bette Davis, striking an artificial stance. 'What good's riding and fighting these days?' he asks angrily. 'Where do they get you?' He works around to expressing his adoration for Davis, boldly seizes her for a tight embrace, then apologizes for his behaviour when she tells him she is doomed to an early death from a brain tumour. While she snatches some last months of happiness in marriage to her doctor (George Brent), Bogart makes one last appearance to remark on her healthy appearance, adding, 'It must be the prayers I've been saying', and spoils her day by reminding her of what lies ahead. The character was as clumsy as Bogart's handling of it!

The Roaring Twenties was a bustling anthology of the gangster film's stock situations as evolved in the thirties –

Above: A traditional western confrontation in *The Oklahoma Kid* (1939) between Bogart and James Cagney

beginning with a variation on the one about the boyhood chums who go their different ways in later life. In the opening scene on a World War I battlefield Jeffrey Lynn acts noble by not picking off a German soldier who looks a mere boy of fifteen, while Bogart shows *his* character by looking along his rifle, squeezing the trigger and announcing: 'He won't be sixteen.' The third soldier, James Cagney, comes somewhere in between. He joins Bogart in the rackets of the Prohibition era when he can't find honest work, then drops out. He comes back to deal with Bogart when the latter threatens the life of Lynn, who also worked in the rackets but is now a crusading crime fighter. Bogart realizes Cagney is a threat but is not quick enough. He raises his hands and retreats, quaking with fear, desperately grabbing an ornament to fling at Cagney, and being shot. He slides down the wall, murmuring, 'Crazy! Crazy!' before Cagney shuts him up for good with two more blasts from his gun.

As in *Oklahoma Kid* (and *Angels with Dirty Faces*), Cagney and Bogart work in conflicting styles that enhance the drama: Cagney full of restless vitality, open and direct; Bogart more intense and controlled, his anger spilling out in sudden eruptions. Incidents highlight this: when his last cigarette is knocked out of his hand by Cagney crashing down on him in the foxhole; when he recognizes his old sergeant (Joe Sawyer) in the raid on the liquor warehouse and (with a sidelit look of crazed glee) happily pumps two bullets into him; or when he pulls out a gun to threaten Jeffrey Lynn, then calms down to issue a warning in the slick gaudy idiom that characterizes the film: 'Listen, Harvard, you came into this racket with your eyes open. You know a lot, you learned a lot. If any of it gets out, you'll go out with your eyes open, only this time they'll have pennies on them!' In the scene on the liquor boat, where Cagney and Bogart forge their partnership, the former walks around while Bogart sits: it's partly the supporting player deferring to the star (the audience watches the one that moves), but is also expressive of their natures.

Last and weirdest of Bogart's 1939 films was *The Return of Doctor X*. No role ever gave Bogart better cause to blanch, both on screen as a blood-starved vampire and off screen for the insult such casting paid to his established abilities.

Perhaps it was one of Jack Warner's punishments; Bogart claimed he used it to lever a raise in salary. Once again, he refused to be ruffled and made the most of the part. And, despite the ridicule usually attached to this film in surveys of Bogart's career, it should be stated that it was a decent horror programmer.

Bogart is Marshall Quesne, assistant to a famous haematologist (John Litel). Eerily lit, he makes his first appearance in the film in white laboratory gown, clutching a rabbit, and extending a cold, clammy hand to shake that of the doctor

Below: In *King of the Underworld* (1939) Bogart studies a book on Napoleon, watched by John Harmon

47

hero (Dennis Morgan). His white-streaked hair, shiney marble-like pallor, calm emotion-drained speech and excessively polite manner elicit the professional observation from Morgan that Bogart is 'a strange-looking creature'. Morgan later goes further, classifying his appearance as a 'cold graveyard look'. But then the level of scientific discussion has been set by John Litel himself, murmuring, 'Interesting stuff, blood', as he shakes a few test tubes.

Bogart is eventually exposed as none other than a former 'medical genius', Dr Francis Xavier, who was electrocuted by the state for letting his investigative zeal run away with him: he killed a baby experimenting to see how long it could survive without food! Now Bogart, who was revived by Litel, can only stay alive by draining blood from suitable victims, one of whom (Rosemary Lane) he abducts to his ramshackle laboratory in some misty swampland in New Jersey. As they drive along, he sits dressed in cloak and trilby and flexes his gloved fingers, looking especially pasty-faced, while Rosemary Lane finally realizes that she's going to put the colour back into his face. Fortunately, the girl's boyfriend (Wayne Morris) and the police are hot on Bogart's trail and shoot him dead at the laboratory, rather flatly terminating his incursion into territory normally reserved for George Zucco and John Carradine.

Invisible Stripes (1940) returned Bogart to familiar ground. Under Lloyd Bacon's careless direction, he and George Raft play parallel scenes as convicts receiving the governor's standard lecture before they are released, and Bogart devastatingly displays his superior acting ability. Raft provides an exaggerated picture of contriteness and keenness to reform, foolishly relaxing his usual deadpan demeanour; Bogart breezes in after him, barely concealing his arrogance and contempt, expressing the essence of hardened criminality. Subsequently, Raft tries to go straight but finds his 'invisible stripes' make it impossible. Bogart returns happily to a life of crime and welcomes Raft as a confederate in a series of bank hold-ups. Raft is acting altruistically, to make some money and keep his discontented younger brother (William Holden) from turning to crime. Bogart is not especially evil: crime is just his way of making a living. Both pay the price in the prescribed manner.

Virginia City (1940) was a noisy, overblown Civil War Western, and Bogart donned the black garments of villainy, sported a proper moustache for the second and last time in his career, and wrestled with a Mexican accent as a half-breed, John Murrell, whose 'beezness' is banditry. Errol Flynn represented the North, Randolph Scott stood for the Confederacy, and Bogart was the one who kept making the mistake of trying to get the better of them, attempting to hold up Flynn and to relieve Scott of a gold shipment; the last is his fatal mistake. Bogart sounded like Speedy Gonzales and demonstrated again that accents were not his forte; besides which, the part really

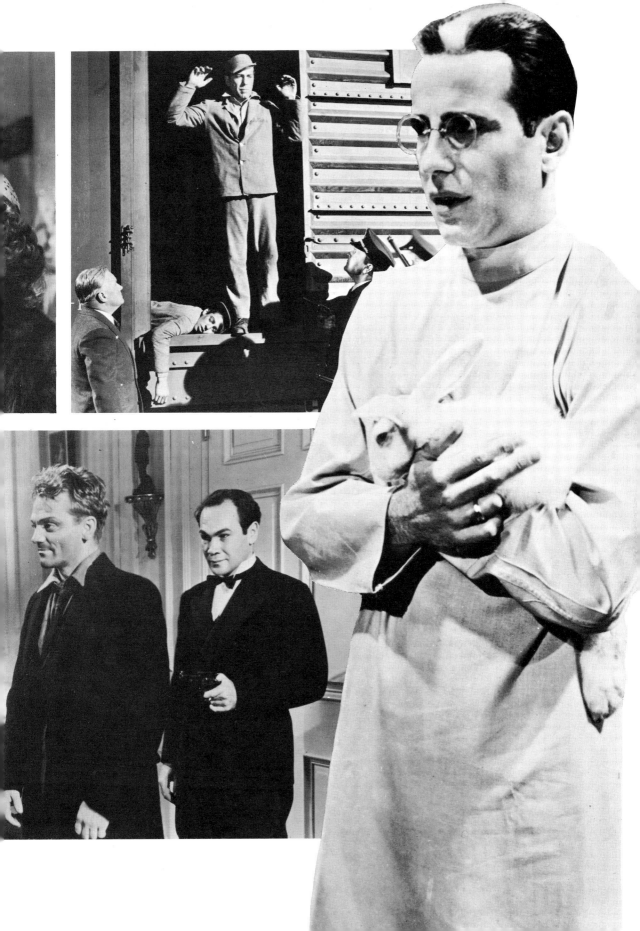

needed a genuine Mexican villain of the type that Hollywood subsequently discovered in Alfonso Bedoya.

In a whimsical oddity called *It All Came True* (1940), Bogart was a gambler and night club operator who hides out from the police in a Victorian boarding house run by two sweet old ladies and largely occupied by non-paying guests from the theatrical profession, who are permanently 'between engagements'. Bogart turns the place into a Gay Nineties club, puts the boarders back to work, and thereby reveals his whereabouts to the police. Ann Sheridan and Jeffrey Lynn had billing ahead of Bogart as a singer and songwriter who help the show to succeed.

Brother Orchid (1940) was one of the Warner studio's periodic gangster spoofs. Like such predecessors as *Little Giant* and *A Slight Case of Murder*, it starred Edward G. Robinson as the gang leader who turns over a new leaf. Here, he hands over to the boys, led by Humphrey Bogart's Jack Buck, and embarks on a European cultural spree. Destitute after five years of high living, he wires the boys to expect him back. Led by a smiling Bogart, they lay out the red carpet and usher him into his old seat at the head of the table, where they've wired up a little surprise to give him the news that he's

Above: Bogart was none too happily cast as a half-breed bandit in *Virginia City* (1940), here with Guinn 'Big Boy' Williams, Errol Flynn and Alan Hale

Inset: In *It All Came True* (1940) Bogart as a hunted criminal is looked after by two sweet old ladies—in this picture Una O'Connor

Previous page above left: In *Dark Victory* (1939) Bogart makes clumsy advances towards his doomed mistress, played by Bette Davis

Above centre: *You Can't Get Away with Murder* (1939)

Right: Bogart as he appeared in *The Return of Doctor X* (1939)

Below: *The Roaring Twenties* (1939)

HUMPHREY BOGART · CONRAD VEIDT · KAAREN VERNE

IN A WARNER BROS. FIRST NATIONAL PICTURE

ALL THROUGH THE NIGHT

Presented by WARNER BROS.

The Big Shot

Humphrey BOGART

Above: The nudge in the
ribs is less than friendly
in this confrontation
between Edward G.
Robinson and Bogart in
Brother Orchid (1940)

through. Robinson tries setting up a rival mob and is nearly
bumped off by Bogart. The film's comic highlights showed
Robinson taking refuge in a monastery and being converted
to its way of life. However, Bogart isn't entirely forgotten: he
gets such a grip on the city market that the monastery is unable
to sell its flowers, so Robinson sets forth, corners Bogart and
pounds him into surrender in a colourful fracas.

Given a rare sympathetic role as a happily married truck-
driver, Bogart inevitably seemed somewhat subdued in Raoul
Walsh's vigorous melodrama, *They Drive By Night* (1940). He
and George Raft were brothers running a private haulage
business and driving all hours to keep up the payments on
their vehicle. Raft, a bachelor, enjoys the life and Bogart goes
along with his views. Though he yearns to spend more time at
home with his wife (Gale Page), he refuses her plea that he
should allow their truck to be reclaimed by the finance company. But Bogart dozes off behind the wheel and wrecks their
truck, losing an arm in the process. Thereafter, Bogart is only
glimpsed, slowly rallying from a bout of depression, while
Raft flirts with Ann Sheridan and is chased by Ida Lupino who
murders her husband (Alan Hale) to make herself free for
him. Eventually, Raft re-establishes himself in business and
makes Bogart his transport manager.

Previous page: Lobby cards
for *All Through the Night*
(above) and *The Big Shot*
(below)

Left: Stephen Humphrey
Bogart is admired by his
parents early in 1949

53

6. THE TURNING POINT

High Sierra (1941) gave Bogart the big break that might have come years earlier at any other studio. But the pecking order at Warners was so long that Bogart was only given roles that Cagney, Robinson, Raft, Garfield and Muni didn't want. All are said to have turned down the opportunity of playing Roy Earle in this W. R. Burnett-John Huston script: Raft because he didn't want to die and he didn't think his fans (or his mother) would like it; Muni because Raft had been offered it first; and so on. Their loss was Bogart's gain – except that, despite having the major role, he had to take second billing to the fast-rising Ida Lupino.

The film is quite simply a glorification of the American gangster, a sentimental tribute on the occasion of his apparent passing from the American scene. It is here rather than in *The Petrified Forest* that Bogart earns Leslie Howard's toast as 'the last great apostle of rugged individualism'. Bogart is a completely sympathetic figure – significantly, the film pays no attention to the crimes that have put him in jail at the start of the film. He is sprung through the efforts of Big Mac (Donald MacBride), who, laid up in a bedroom far away slowly dying, needs Bogart to carry out one last big caper for him. As Bogart walks out of prison, he rejects the seat in a waiting car and communes with nature (walking in a park, tossing a ball back to some kids) and with his past (a call at the farm where he was brought up). He befriends a simple, tiresome oldtimer (Henry Travers) who is taking his family across the country in an old jalopy and intervenes on their behalf when they cause a minor road accident.

Bogart is not only decent but loyal. He reassures MacBride: 'I never let nobody down – you know that.' Their reunion is more sad than joyful. 'All the good guys are gone – dead or in Alcatraz,' laments MacBride. 'Not many of the old bunch left,' comments the old doctor, played by Henry Hull. 'Sometimes I feel I don't know what it's all about any more,' adds Bogart.

When he later leads the raid on the Tropico Inn, working with youngsters he doesn't trust, he does it more to meet his obligation to MacBride than to resume a life of crime. When he shoots and kills a policeman, the latter has fired first and so it is (from Bogart's point of view, with which we identify) a case of self-defence. When Bogart subsequently finds himself labelled 'Mad Dog' Earle by the newspapers, he is disgusted and indignant: one might think the bad image of gangsters was entirely a press invention.

Here Bogart is such a sentimental figure he hasn't the heart to abandon a stray dog and he digs into his own pocket so that a young girl (Joan Leslie) can be cured of a club foot. He hopes that her gratitude will lead to love, idealizing her prettiness and youth. Her rejection of his marriage proposal is a hard blow to Bogart's hope and turns into a grievous insult when her choice of fiancé proves to be an unprepossessing, nearly

High Sierra (1941): Bogart with Ida Lupino, who played the dance hall girl who really loved him. The crumpled newspaper is the one that brands him as 'Mad Dog' Earle

middle-aged figure. Hung up on society's standards of decency, he is slow to appreciate the real loyalty of Marie (Ida Lupino), the dance-hall girl who is deeply responsive to the kindness he has shown her.

It is symptomatic of the film's elegiac regard for the Bogart character that it should be his noble qualities that are his undoing. He refuses to be reimbursed by the crippled girl's fiancé for the operation and so has no funds to buy petrol; this forces him to hold up a store and put the police on his tail. Cornered in the High Sierra mountains, he responds to the barks of the stray dog racing up towards him and comes out far enough to be picked off by a marksman. It is this marksman who carries out the film's real act of heroism, calmly climbing where no one has ever climbed before to get his sights on Bogart (of course, shooting him in the back rather undermines the effect). As Bogart lies dead, the dog licks his hand, then Ida Lupino caresses it as bystanders comment that he doesn't look much any more. Weeping bitterly, Lupino has the consolation that Bogart has 'crashed out' to freedom in the next world.

Why, one might ask, is this specious and maudlin picture so effective? One reason is that Raoul Walsh's direction does not dwell on the sentimental side but remains detached, emphasizing speed, conflict and action, while Bogart never plays for pathos. In fact, Bogart's performance is remarkably astute. Far from a glamour figure, he looks older than his actual years in a dark, crumpled suit, battered felt hat, loose collar, and 'pudding bowl' prison haircut. He resists the temptation of enlarging this forlorn appearance into his concept of the character; he keeps going, surrendering neither to the police nor to an introspective awareness of his symbolic function. A further reason is that *High Sierra*'s fondness for its tragic hero gangster mirrors the audience's basic liking for the genre – especially today when time has made the thirties remote and ripe for nostalgia. We are not drawn into moral judgements, not seriously anyway, so *High Sierra* offers much to enjoy.

With it, Bogart himself 'crashed out' from supporting parts to become a valuable asset of the Warner acting stable, and leading man material. *High Sierra*'s success made it possible for John Huston to direct his next script, *The Maltese Falcon*, and obtain Bogart for the lead once George Raft had turned it down for fear of entrusting himself to an untried director.

Before that, however, Bogart said his farewell to the routine picture with *The Wagons Roll at Night* (1941), an ingenious re-working of *Kid Galahad* with Bogart's old gangster role eliminated, the boxing background changed to a travelling carnival, and Bogart stepping up into the lead formerly taken by Edward G. Robinson. Here the emphasis was more on the leading character's Achilles' heel, his latent incestuous regard for his younger sister whom he has had raised in a convent to keep her 'clean and decent'. He regards the entertainers who

Above: Bogart, as private eye Sam Spade in *The Maltese Falcon* (1941), watches Mary Astor, his mysterious client, thank his secretary—Lee Patrick—for an offer of help

work in his carnival as 'roadshow vermin' unfit to have any contact with her. When a young lion tamer (Eddie Albert, equivalent to the boxer in *Kid Galahad*) falls in love with her, and Bogart's own girl, a fortune-teller (Sylvia Sidney), takes a shine to the lad, Bogart plots to send him unarmed into a cage with a killer lion. In a last minute change of heart, he rushes forward and is mauled instead: a few dark smudges on his face suggest his injuries, as he dies, regretting his jealousy and blessing his sister's romance with the lion tamer. Bogart was good in the part. The confident manipulation of people, the flashes of irritation, the devious scheming for revenge (one memorable shot of him with his eyes glinting as the mad lion roars nearby) were contrasted with more sympathetic moments like his subtly registered panic at the prospect of losing Sylvia Sidney after he has come to depend on her being around.

But it was as private investigator Sam Spade in *The Maltese Falcon* (1941) that Bogart at last found a part that really called for the particular qualities he could offer – including, at that time, a basic ambiguity about his moral position. Bogart seemed to be the hero but didn't always act like it, and was stamped in the eyes of screen audiences as a villain.

The Maltese Falcon is a particularly honest detective film. Like the later *The Big Sleep*, it restricts us with fleeting exceptions to scenes in which Bogart participates, so that we uncover the facts as he does, and watch him closely to see how he responds to them. Unlike *The Big Sleep*, however, the plot eventually makes complete sense, if you care to work it out.

Bogart as Spade is decent enough to earn the uncritical devotion of his sensible secretary Effie (Lee Patrick) who mothers him and receives his confidences, yet he is not above having an affair with his partner's wife (Gladys George), nor is he particularly disturbed when his partner is murdered, losing no time in removing the man's desk and his name from the office. As he gains a footing in the main intrigue and learns about the precious, jewel-encrusted, golden Maltese falcon, he names himself as an interested party in sharing the spoils. After it falls into his hands, he delivers the 'black bird' to Gutman (Sydney Greenstreet) and the others, but whether he is working for monetary gain or to clear up the case is a debatable point. 'Don't be so sure I'm as crooked as I seem to be,' he declares at one point, and at the end he indicates that solving his partner's murder is a factor motivating his conduct.

Bogart certainly succumbs to the atmosphere of greedy excitement that surrounds the prized object. He exultantly grips Effie's wrist until it hurts when receiving the falcon from the dying Captain Jacobi, and he savours the thrill that Gutman and his colleagues derive from unwrapping the falcon after he has handed it over to them.

In the 1931 version, Ricardo Cortez played Sam Spade as a

Below : In *The Big Shot* (1942) Bogart stages a jailbreak helped by Chick Chandler, a prisoner in costume for a concert. Richard Travis occupies the floor

suave ladies' man who lived and worked in plush surroundings. Here Bogart is an older man with none of the romantic aura he was later to acquire. His nondescript clothes, his spacious, sunny but bare office, his gloomy and anonymous apartment – these give us an impression of a man who has got little from life. He is interested in Brigid O'Shaughnessy (Mary Astor) as a client because she is an alluring and classy dame who is clearly involved in something far bigger than the small-time work he normally handles.

When she asks how she can keep his help when she has no money, Bogart seizes her for a kiss. His brutish, dominating manner – putting his hands around her neck, impressing his thumbs into her cheeks, holding her head still for the kiss – was to become his standard technique as a screen lover, but here it suggests a certain crude eagerness and a lack of sophistication. Later Bogart determines to extract the truth about the falcon from her but he allows himself to be diverted into making love. At the end of the film, Bogart stampedes the truth out of her – that she is a cold-blooded murderess. Here his acting reaches its greatest intensity as his reasoning battles with his emotions, and he denies the burning impulse to save her as she implores him to do. His angry 'I won't play the sap for you' contrasts with his melancholic 'I hope they don't hang you, precious, for that sweet neck' (he gently touches it) and his consoling 'If they hang you, I'll always remember you'. Aided by the harsh lighting, Bogart looks really haggard as he speaks of the sleepless nights he'll have until time erodes the pain of losing her. His final decision – 'I won't because all of me wants to' – carries a hint of indignation that he should have come so close to surrendering to impulse, but the overall tone is one of savage bitterness.

Above: Gambler Bogart and Nazi leader Conrad Veidt at odds in *All Through the Night* (1942)

Throughout, Bogart's performance is tremendously alert and scene after scene is enhanced by his handling of details, as well as by the marvellous performances contributed by the rest of an extraordinary cast. Bogart's toothy smile as he takes Brigid's excessively large retainer in his office; his humorous mimicking of Peter Lorre's Joel Cairo ('I will take, say, *two* hundred') as he accepts money from him; his effort to shake himself awake as the telephone pierces the still of night with the news of his partner's death; the puzzled reaction to a drugged drink as he shakes his head and tries to remain conscious; the way he turns his head slowly to look at Brigid after one of Gutman's remarks shows her to him in her real colours, and the subsequent smile he gives her as he gently disarms her of the gun he now knows she is fully capable of using: all these and more contribute to a remarkably rounded impression of a man. Had the part been played as flatly as one must imagine George Raft would have handled it, *The Maltese Falcon* would probably have been a thorough bore with its complications of plot, whereas Bogart fully maintains the

interest of the audience because he is so visibly interested.

All Through the Night (1942) demonstrated Bogart's improved standing at Warners: he was now the leading man in a big picture, indeed the only star name in the cast. The part of Broadway gambler Gloves Donahue wasn't exactly tailored to his abilities but then these were in the process of being established now that he was relieved of playing villains. The studio tried for a more youthful look – he sported a fuller head of hair – and gave him some athletic heroics in this spirited contribution to the war effort. It was a merry, Runyonesque comedy pitting Bogart and his cronies against a band of Fifth Columnists plotting acts of sabotage. Bogart starts out nonchalant about world affairs – 'That's Washington's racket – let them handle it' – but refutes the argument of the Nazi (Conrad Veidt) that they should work together, as neither has any respect for democracy. Bogart admits that he may not be a model citizen but points out that he pays his taxes and buys tickets for the policemen's ball. Eventually Bogart becomes democracy's advocate before his sceptical fellow gamblers and even impresses shady Barton MacLane with the news that the Fascists would dictate what paper he could read; 'Why, that's against the law!' exclaims this veteran screen lawbreaker. The film substitutes speed for subtlety and some good scenes – such as Bogart uttering gibberish, stalling for time, when forced to address a Nazi meeting as a supposed agent – are rather buried in the rush. But a powerful supporting cast, including Jane Darwell, improbably cast as Bogart's domineering mother, help the actor put the action across in a pleasant and entertaining manner.

Below: Bogart, with Monte Blue and Mary Astor, held at gunpoint by Sen Yung in *Across the Pacific* (1942)

With *The Big Shot* (1942) Bogart seemed momentarily to be sliding back towards the kind of film he made before *Falcon*: here he was Duke Berne, a former big shot scared to break the law because his next jail sentence will be life imprisonment. A certain irony develops when Bogart is goaded into taking part in a robbery, then restrained at gunpoint by his girl friend (Irene Manning). Nevertheless, a witness identifies him as one of the robbers and puts him in prison. In a break-out, he has to kill a guard and subsequent sequences, reminiscent of *High Sierra*, depict his desperate flight into the mountains with his girl. She dies in a police ambush while Bogart settles accounts with her husband, the crooked lawyer (Stanley Ridges) who betrayed them, and, mortally wounded, dies clearing a friend who has been charged with the murder of the prison guard. *The Big Shot* is one of the few forgotten pictures of Bogart's star years.

The actor recovered some ground with *Across the Pacific* (1942) in which he was reunited with Mary Astor, Sydney Greenstreet and director John Huston in a laboured but not unentertaining attempt to recapture the success of *The Maltese Falcon*. Bogart teased audiences for a while, by being court-martialled

out of the Army and cultivating the friendship of Greenstreet,
a Japanese agent, as both journey on a freighter to the Far East,
but soon revealed himself as the undercover agent we always
thought he was. Mary Astor was another woman of mystery,
certainly not all she pretends to be, and Bogart directly echoes
his dialogue to her in *Falcon* by complimenting her, 'You're
good, angel, you're very, very good', before demanding the
truth. Their romance is important to Bogart, who describes
her as the kind of woman a young man dreams about, but is
mainly handled as sophisticated comedy. Bogart displays a
deft manner with lines that enable him to be knowingly comic
and exasperating, but the lines themselves are far from brilliant. Sydney Greenstreet stirs the melodramatic stew and
thoroughly outsmarts Bogart, leaving him unconscious on the
floor, just as in *Falcon*, and beaten savagely with a walking
stick (to correspond with Elisha Cook Jr's kicks to his face in
the earlier film).

The plot here never amounts to enough to engage real
interest and is spoiled by lack of thought. Bogart saves Greenstreet from an assassin's bullet but consigns the thwarted
killer to a quick execution (which rather leaves an unnoticed
stain on Bogart's conscience). The hyperbolic climax places
Bogart behind a machine-gun for some Errol Flynn heroics,
mowing down the Jap hordes and writing finis to a far-fetched
scheme to bomb the Panama canal. Huston evidently realized
he was directing an inconsequential potboiler when he worked
Bogart into as tight a spot as possible, then left the film to fight
in the war; the replacement director and a phalanx of writers
struggled for days to effect the hero's escape!

EDWARD G.
ROBINSON
IN
'BROTHER
ORCHID'

7. A CLASSIC CALLED CASABLANCA

Casablanca (1942) is, of course, *the* Bogart film – the quintessential expression of the Bogart character. Though created under the most extraordinary conditions of haste and confusion, with new pages of script being delivered as shooting progressed and players uncertain of the ending, it has the contrary look of a thoughtfully prepared, lovingly crafted romantic melodrama. With a dazzling cast, it never wastes a second under Michael Curtiz's typically swift direction. The result remains a richly satisfying film, both of its time, as rousing anti-Nazi propaganda, and timeless in its feeling for the vicissitudes of love.

As Rick Blaine, Bogart was no certain screen hero but a touchy, stubborn, self-centred figure who couldn't be relied on absolutely to do the right thing. Yet the film also gave a whole new romantic dimension to Bogart as a man who has flung himself wholeheartedly into love and is immensely vulnerable to emotional upsets. From a figure whose few leading ladies had tended to be on the mature side, he became a suitable romantic lead for the much younger Ingrid Bergman – reputedly since all the regular romantic leads were tied up, a good many in fighting the war.

Casablanca's flashback shows us images of a Parisian romance. Bogart is radiantly happy in his whirlwind courtship of Ingrid Bergman, rushing her towards marriage, blind to the troubled look in her eyes and the hesitation in her voice. Her cryptic note of farewell as he hastens from Paris ahead of the German invaders is a stunning blow to his self-esteem as the rain symbolically wipes out the episode by smudging Bergman's cruel, curt writing and represents Bogart's tears.

Previously called Richard Blaine, he becomes 'Rick' of Rick's Place in Casablanca in late 1941: he has hardened like his name, withdrawn into himself. When Yvonne (Madeleine LeBeau) seeks to extend what has obviously been a casual affair by asking where he'll be that evening, Bogart's reply, 'I never make plans that far ahead,' echoes Bergman's 'That's too far ahead to plan' when he urged marriage on her at the earliest opportunity in Paris. When Bogart sharply rebuffs Sydney Greenstreet's attempt (as the black market leader, Signor Ferrari) to buy the services of the club pianist, Sam (Dooley Wilson), his reply not only reflects distaste at the suggestion's parallels with the city's ready bartering of human lives, it is also a reflection of his eagerness to keep Sam, his companion from Paris days, as a ready reminder of the past which, as the reply he gives Yvonne indicates, haunts him closely.

The film economically conveys Bogart's political inclinations despite his professed neutrality. He has fought the Fascists in Spain, and had to leave Paris because the Germans were keen to capture him. His recognition of the type of armour heard booming in the Parisian suburbs is a skilful

Casablanca (1942): romance in Paris in the summer, with Bogart radiantly happy on a boat trip along the Seine in the company of Ingrid Bergman

Overleaf: The airport finale as Claude Rains aids the escape of Paul Henreid and Ingrid Bergman from Casablanca, while Bogart clutches the 'persuader' in his trenchcoat pocket

indication of his military background. Even in Casablanca, he shows a strong and undiplomatic dislike for Germans, ordering one away from his gambling tables and letting the band play *La Marseillaise* to drown out the Germans singing *Wacht am Rhein*, an act which leads to the closure of his club. Bogart is visibly impressed at mention of the resistance leader, Victor Laszlo, and the prefect of police (Claude Rains) realizes he will be tempted to help Laszlo travel on to the free world. Bogart's stated attitude – 'I stick my neck out for no one' – is transparently a case of self-deception. When he refuses to help Ugarte (Peter Lorre) evade capture by the police, it is because it is too late to aid him as he did earlier by hiding the valuable letters of transit that will provide whoever carries them with the perfect means of escape from Casablanca.

Thus almost everything predisposes Bogart to aid Laszlo (played by Paul Henreid). The one stumbling block is the reappearance of Ingrid Bergman as the man's companion. Bogart memorably conveys the impact of her unexpected return with his angry stride to stop Sam playing the tune that recalls Paris, *As Time Goes By*, and his startled, dumbfounded reaction to the sight of her standing there. Then he breaks all precedents by having a drink with her and Henreid. Drinking late at night in a haze of cigarette smoke, he relives the past to help him resist the explanation for her betrayal that he knows she will bring; suspicious that she will only be seeking the letters of transit. It is a losing battle, and when Bergman ultimately seeks to take the precious letters at gunpoint, then breaks down, Bogart is forced to admire her once more, and then to accept her complete submission to his will. Paul Henreid makes Laszlo seem a poor lover compared to Bogart: the very qualities of aloofness and cautious diplomacy that make him a 'great man' deny him the spontaneous, reckless feelings of passionate love, even though he depends on Bergman. His selfless, noble offer to sacrifice his own freedom to ensure hers is admirable, but coldblooded and calculated.

For Bogart, the time has come to act, not react. His ingenious solution to everybody's problems teases us with the possibility that he has betrayed the resistance leader to the police, then enables him to re-stage that unsatisfactory departure from Paris in an equally urgent departure scene at Casablanca's airport, again losing Bergman, but by his choice this time and so with his self-esteem intact. He has now 'betrayed' her, and yet strengthens their bond by doing it for the same reason: the greater cause represented by Henreid as Laszlo. And, in this thoroughly beguiling entertainment, our satisfaction with the climax is compounded by the opportunity it allows Bogart to kill the Nazi leader (Conrad Veidt), after he has honourably but improbably allowed the German to get off the first shot, and to replace the hazards of loving a woman with the more stable, less competitive friendship possible between two

Bogart plunges off a burning tanker in *Action in the North Atlantic* (1943)

men like Bogart and Claude Rains, as fellow patriots who thoroughly enjoy each other's company.

Bogart gained an Academy Award nomination for best actor but lost to Paul Lukas, who also fought the Fascists (but more seriously) in *Watch on the Rhine*.

Any rugged actor from the studio ranks would have done for the role Bogart played in his next film, *Action in the North Atlantic*. Despite solo billing ahead of the title, he largely plays a subordinate role as first mate to Raymond Massey's Captain Jarvis on a merchant ship making hazardous crossings during wartime. Bogart's Joe Rossi is a simple-minded, fun-loving fellow who has to be rescued from the women he meets by Massey. Then he silences a loudmouth who is interrupting the singer in a particularly desolate-looking bar and ends up married to her. At sea, he is conscientious and respectful and considers himself too easygoing to command. He has sailed into Axis ports and didn't like what he saw, but isn't enormously steamed up about it. The film depicts how he changes, becoming under the pressure of events an able captain in place of the wounded Massey (whose leg he successfully operates on), outwitting a German submarine and conducting a funeral service with quiet dignity, emphasizing the obligation of those that live to make the sacrifice of the dead a worthwhile one. As their international convoy reaches the Russians, (then, of course, our valued allies), Bogart strangely casts a shadow across the celebratory tone of the sequence by contemplating the hazards of the journey back. The film is excellent propaganda and its action sequences are remarkable, quite dwarfing Bogart's competent performance.

Sahara (1943) was a more conventional war film, derived in part from a Russian film and scripted, like *Action in the North Atlantic*, by John Howard Lawson, later to become one of the Hollywood Ten accused of putting Communist propaganda on the screen. No case was ever proved, and *Sahara* owes more to *The Lost Patrol* and others of that ilk than to the Soviets.

Bogart was the sergeant commanding a tank called Lulubelle in the Libyan desert after the fall of Tobruk. In the general retreat, he and his crew of two take on a number of passengers forming the usual international cross-section – English, French, Sudanese, South African and Irish from our side, plus German and Italian prisoners. The main quest is to find water. They reach a waterhole just ahead of a huge contingent of thirsty Germans and decide to defend it. Eventually, Bogart is one of only two survivors and he shouts final defiance at the Germans as they surge forward in a huge wave, only to find they are intent on surrendering to him. *Sahara* communicated a powerful sense of the harsh, arid desert terrain through Rudolph Maté's bleached, dusty images. As in Bogart's previous film, characterization ran a poor second to spectacle. Bogart was a decent, average guy whose home is the

Sahara (1943): Bogart as the American tank commander in the Libyan Desert, with Patrick O'Moore in the background

Overleaf: In *Passage to Marseille* (1943) Bogart is sickened to see the German aircraft have gunned down the mess boy (Billy Roy)

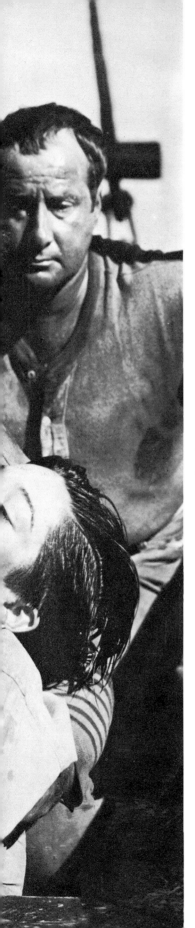

army. In a film espousing group effort, it was only right that he should not stand out, though he was the sole star name in the cast. However, in his address to the men, persuading them to stay and fight the Germans, his performance does strike a distinctive note through the controlled intensity of his argument.

Passage to Marseille (1944) was Bogart's third contribution to the war effort and represented some wishful thinking on the Brothers Warner's part, that putting most of the stars and the director of *Casablanca* to work on a shallow script might produce something of the same popular appeal. Though Michael Curtiz and cameraman James Wong Howe invest the film with striking, moody images, the script's complicated structure and rudimentary characterization prevent it from meaning much. Bogart plays a crusading French journalist, Jean Matrac (he wisely attempts no accent), who opposes appeasement at Munich in 1938; his premature hatred of Fascism leads to his incarceration on Devil's Island on a trumped-up murder charge. He escapes with other convicts and alone remains silent while they affirm their patriotism and promise to fight for their country in the war against Germany.

Bogart makes a frighteningly intense and humourless figure out of Matrac. His romance with Michele Morgan's Paula is perfunctorily developed and interrupted by political events. It never has the impact of the Paris scenes in *Casablanca*. His disillusionment with his country while on Devil's Island is vividly etched in scenes of him striding up and down his cell, railing against the injustice that has brought him there. He coldbloodedly murders a prisoner who tries to horn in on their escape. On board the freighter, he tells Captain Freycinet (Claude Rains) that he has no intention of fighting for France and only intends returning to Paula, who became his wife.

But when Major Duval (Sydney Greenstreet) takes over the ship, the twitch in Bogart's right cheek, the only movement in his otherwise impassively grim face, foretells of trouble for the Fascist sympathizer. Bogart helps overthrow Duval and guns down the German plane that attacks the ship, wounding both the mess boy and one of his fellow escaped convicts (Peter Lorre). When Bogart spots survivors from the crashed plane drifting in the water, he rushes along the deck to a machine-gun and fires on them. The ship's captain (Victor Francen) protests, and Bogart's subsequent death from wounds received as a gunner on a bombing raid over Germany is a delayed form of retribution. Bogart's unbridled fanaticism makes him useful rather than admirable: he needs to commit himself totally to a cause, as he did in politics before the war. Even his last letter to his son, read at a bleakly shot clifftop funeral, is more an outlet for his fervent beliefs than the spontaneous feelings of a loving father. Thus Matrac hints at other dark figures to come in the gallery of Bogart characters whose deep-seated emotions get the better of them.

8. BOGART MEETS BACALL

To *Have and Have Not* (1944) paired Bogart, then in his mid-forties, with a newcomer named Lauren Bacall, then aged nineteen. It was the final stage in the remarkable evolution of Bogart's romantic image from the days when he was a sour-faced heavy. Their scenes together were electric. Today, they retain an impact but their effect is more comic than sensual; originally the balance would have been the other way round. Director Howard Hawks realized the only way to make sense of their disparity in age was to have the girl dominate Bogart and have Bogart allow it because he enjoys her extravagant performance. The rest of the film was a superficial reworking of the situations in *Casablanca*, with aspects of the Ernest Hemingway novel (which gave the film its title) tacked on.

Here was Bogart as Harry Morgan, an adventurer in French territory – Martinique – seeking to remain neutral after the fall of France. In *Casablanca*, he parried Conrad Veidt's question about his nationality by calling himself a drunkard; here he responds to equally tiresome and unnecessary probing by declaring himself an Eskimo before becoming more co-operative. Here he declines to become involved in what he calls 'local politics' just as he ignored the underground in *Casablanca*. 'What are your sympathies?' he is asked. 'Minding my own business,' he replies. Just as Claude Rains advanced as a reason for Bogart to help Laszlo his dislike for Veidt's Nazi, so here it finds its echo in Bogart's explanation for finally undertaking a hazardous trip for the Resistance to free a patriot imprisoned on Devil's Island: 'Maybe because I like you and I don't like them.'

In characteristic Hawks manner, broad issues never matter compared to personal relationships. Bogart first works for the Resistance in order to buy a plane ticket to dispatch Slim (Lauren Bacall) to safety. He keeps Walter Brennan's Eddie on the payroll because he was once a good man. When he hires out his boat to a tourist for deep-sea fishing, he vicariously shares his client's excitement as he tries to haul in a big fish, hands rubbing his thighs as he gives him precise instructions, but openly betrays his vexation when the man fumbles his opportunity. But even more exasperating is the Vichy police chief (Dan Seymour) whose rough questioning of Bacall prompts Bogart to step forward – 'Go ahead, slap *me*!' he challenges one of the chief's men. Then, when the chief gets rough with Walter Brennan, Bogart really explodes, turning the tables on Seymour, pistol-whipping him into arranging Brennan's release over the telephone.

But such scenes are eclipsed by the love scenes and the fame of such lines as 'If you want me, just whistle.' In actual fact that line is a little more complicated. It follows Bacall kissing Bogart and remarking, 'It's even better when you help,' then declaring 'You know you don't have to act with me, Steve. You

The Big Sleep (1946): Bogart in a tender but possessive moment with Lauren Bacall, co-star and off-screen wife

Overleaf left: In *To Have and Have Not* (1944) Bogart, as an American who wants to remain neutral in German-occupied Martinique, argues with the Vichy police chief (Dan Seymour). Watching are Sheldon Leonard, Lauren Bacall, Aldo Nadi

Overleaf right: In the same film Bogart talks to Marcel Dalio, French patriot and underground leader. Behind Bogart is Walter Brennan

don't have to say anything and you don't have to do anything. Not a thing. Oh, maybe just *whistle*. You know how to whistle, don't you, Steve? You just put your lips together – and *blow*.' As she leaves him, Bogart experimentally puts his lips together, lets out a low whistle, and smiles to himself. Bacall's coaching of Bogart follows from her awareness that he has been badly burnt by a woman, and their scenes are loaded with fire symbolism – lighting matches, smoking cigarettes, exhaling smoke.

The effect on the box-office was equally inflammatory and they were hurriedly reteamed for *The Big Sleep*, filmed in January 1945. On May 21 of that year, eleven days after Bogart's divorce from Mayo Methot became final, Bogart married Bacall. Curiously, *The Big Sleep* was not released until more than a year after their marriage (although production was resumed to increase their footage together). Instead, audiences saw Lauren Bacall in *Confidential Agent* and Bogart in *Conflict* (1945).

Actually, *Conflict* had been made in mid-1943 just before *Passage to Marseille*. Like other Warner films, it seems to have been stockpiled after a frenzy of activity in 1942/43 to ensure a steady flow later when war-time difficulties might have curbed production. It was certainly a rather curious film for Bogart to be seen in after *To Have and Have Not*, casting him as a wife murderer who inadvertently reveals his guilt to a psychologist

(Sydney Greenstreet). The latter contrives an ingenious (i.e. thoroughly far-fetched) scheme to worry Bogart into returning to the scene of his crime by making him think his wife is still alive, thereby displaying his guilt to the waiting police.

In the film, Bogart disposes of his shrewish wife (Rose Hobart) because he loves her younger sister (Alexis Smith), and it is possible to see milder parallels in Bogart's own life, his marital switch to a much younger woman, and in his changing screen image, moving towards younger, more glamorous romantic partners. Here, though, Bogart is not allowed to reap any happiness from his murder; Alexis Smith does not fall into his arms. The part gained much from Bogart's ability to convey nervous agitation. The way in which he frightens the landlady of an empty apartment, into which a woman resembling his wife has vanished, or tries to hector Alexis Smith into loving him, prefigures the murderous rages and desperate needs of his Dixon Steele in *In a Lonely Place*. Though Bogart is well cast, the film is a minor melodrama that, without him, would have vanished into obscurity.

In *The Big Sleep* (1946), Bogart portrayed Raymond Chandler's tough private eye, Philip Marlowe, in an intrigue so labyrinthine that it made *The Maltese Falcon* look like a nursery rhyme. Bogart uncovers a plot involving gambling, pornography, blackmail and murder, and during his travels encounters a bevy of beautiful women: even his taxi-driver is female and willing, while a prim-looking woman (Dorothy Malone) closes her bookshop early and lets down her hair to spend an hour over a bottle of rye with the private investigator. The only woman who takes a dim view of his antics is Agnes (Sonia Darrin) but then he does antagonize her with a bizarre appearance as a phoney hunter of rare books in the antiquarian bookshop: a pair of spectacles rests on the end of his nose, his hat brim is turned up, his voice breathless and effeminate.

Much of the film is devoted to slick banter, particularly with Bacall, who starts things off between them by responding to her first sight of Bogart with: 'My, you're a mess, aren't you!' Bogart responds: 'I'm not very tall either. Next time I'll come on stilts.' Bacall is an enigmatic figure, clearly involved in the cover-up of whatever is being covered up, as apt to mention Marcel Proust as display a provocative leg, but mostly having fun in such engaging tomfoolery as teasing a police sergeant over the telephone with Bogart's help.

Bogart also trades smart answers with such figures as Eddie Mars (John Ridgely) who threatens to make Bogart's business his business. 'You wouldn't like it,' Bogart tells him. 'The pay's too small.' But eventually the fun stops as Bogart stubbornly refuses to be paid off, and gives a classic justification: 'Too many people told me to stop.' He encounters in Bob Steele's Canino one of the meanest adversaries ever to populate the crime film: Canino poisons a doughty private eye

Right: *Conflict* (1945): A puzzled Bogart gazes at a portrait of the wife he has murdered and at a letter apparently written by her and posted since her death

Overleaf
Left: In *The Big Sleep* (1946) Bogart puts on an act in an antiquarian bookshop that is a front for blackmail and pornography

Above: His chin bruised, Bogart is given a cigarette and is about to be further helped out of a tight spot by Lauren Bacall

Below: In *Dead Reckoning* (1947) Bogart displays his typical screen manner with a woman (here it's Lizabeth Scott); it's hard to tell whether he planned to choke her or kiss her

Right: Bogart and Tim Holt in *The Treasure of the Sierra Madre* (1948) in which both played eager but inexperienced gold prospectors. This rare colour shot gives an idea of what the film would have looked like had it not been photographed in monochrome

(another of Elisha Cook Jr's unfortunate losers) and is taken very seriously indeed by Bogart, who memorably characterizes him as the kind of man who'd knock all your teeth out and then punch you in the stomach for mumbling. In their final confrontation, Bogart dispenses with the usual screen formality of allowing the other side to get off the first shot and shoots Canino before he can fire. Bogart's showdown with John Ridgely is presented as another gruellingly dangerous experience, making *The Big Sleep* doubly satisfactory as a fun picture that turns into a gripping action thriller.

Dead Reckoning (1947) was rushed into production at Columbia when Bogart was suddenly made available to repay Harry Cohn for stars he had lent much earlier. Cohn wanted his top female star, Rita Hayworth, to play opposite Bogart, but they were feuding over her contract and Lizabeth Scott had to be borrowed from Hal B. Wallis at Paramount. Bogart had director approval and accepted John Cromwell, whom he had known in his Broadway days.

For some reason, *Dead Reckoning* has quite a reputation as a Bogart picture and *film noir*. Seen today, it belongs to the worst variety of slick, phoney, hardboiled melodrama, with Bogart sounding like an arrested adolescent trying to talk tough as he relates his story to an incredibly patient priest and provides narrative to introduce flashbacks that show him investigating the mysterious disappearance and death of a wartime buddy. The gaudier the patter, the cheaper the picture – to paraphrase one of the Bogart's lines in *The Maltese Falcon* – and this was as cheap as they come. Lizabeth Scott was another deceitful heroine who, like Mary Astor in *Falcon*, earns Bogart's 'You're awfully good' rating for her lies; but Astor was a much better actress. The regular villains are nasty without style: indeed, all the violence is rather unpalatable. Even the images lack the sheen and shadow of the best Warner product.

Far more entertaining – if equally dreadful on any scale of artistic achievement – was *The Two Mrs Carrolls* (1947), which gave Bogart his most lunatic role since *The Return of Doctor X*. As a wife murderer in *Conflict* he'd been fairly sane and had a conventional motive; here he's a painter who kills old wives and marries new ones to get the creative juices flowing again. As always, Bogart gave a dedicated performance, erupting into a characteristic expression of rage in his studio attic, tapping his brush, flinging down his cigarette and wiping the canvas clean of unsatisfactory work. Periodically, he fingers his right temple as a sign of mental disarray, and when his daughter mentions the insanity of Van Gogh to him, he stiffens, seizes the book she is reading, and feverishly strokes that temple again! When he finds wife number two (Barbara Stanwyck) has thrown away her poisoned milk and rumbled his intentions, he feels *both* temples as fair warning of his rainsoaked appearance at her bedroom window. While she

Bogart chats between takes on *Key Largo* (1948) with Felipa Gomez, who was introduced in the film as an ancient Indian woman

Previous page : Bogart is seen with Carl Benton Reid, to whom he confesses that his priestly garb is a masquerade, in *The Left Hand of God* (1955). Don Forbes is seen in the background

desperately calls the police, his arms stretch out to thrust the curtains apart, like a vampire on a gleeful nocturnal call.

Director Peter Godfrey earlier makes Bogart telegraph his madness with sinisterly lit eye-bulging, pupil-darting and face-quivering close-ups. He also lays on the atmosphere of a leafy English cathedral town far too heavily, and introduces a dreadful mismatch when Bogart is strangling Stanwyck on her bed; in one shot, his face trembling with the effort; in a close-up, perfectly still. He never even makes Alexis Smith seem inspirational enough to warrant doing away with Stanwyck.

Bogart's last appearance, being led away by the police, carries a frank admission of the absurdity of it all, as Bogart is allowed to turn and ask his two escorts, 'Would you gentlemen like a drink? A glass of *milk*, perhaps?' Warners, who also encouraged Peter Godfrey to play around with Errol Flynn's image in *Cry Wolf* (1947), had a big investment to recover since *The Two Mrs Carrolls* had been a hit play, but it seems a most curious use of Bogart. The film was actually made just after *The Big Sleep* but shelved for two years – obviously to space it away from Bogart's other uxoricidal work in *Conflict*.

Dark Passage (1947) is the most tender of the Bogart-Bacall films, a beguiling and offbeat romantic drama. Superficially, Bogart is completely wrong for the part: as a convicted wife-murderer (but this time actually innocent), he breaks out of San Quentin and spends most of the film vainly trying to master his fate and being dependent on others. He especially relies on Lauren Bacall, a wealthy artist who has convinced herself of his innocence and remains true to him even when he seems responsible for two further deaths. For her, helping Bogart is a way of getting even with society for her father's fate (he died in prison, also convicted of wife murder) and Bogart is

a substitute father figure on whom to lavish her concern. Her psychological need of him is balanced by his sense of gratitude towards her (and, doubtless, appreciation of her good looks) and this is a basis for their lasting happiness.

In this film, the Bogart face is a disguise created by a plastic surgeon. Writer-director Delmer Daves ingeniously uses a great deal of subjective camerawork to avoid showing Bogart before he looks like Bogart. We hear the familiar voice and see a different face in the newspapers so that we know his looks have been changed. It is, in fact, more than an hour into the film before the bandages come off and Bogart peers at his unshaven features, full of curiosity as to what he will see.

The film is about faith (Bogart's) and charity (that of others). Bogart has his moments of doubt as the surgeon fingers his razor and contemplates the range of possibilities open to him; his eyes signal alarm as Lauren Bacall seems to be betraying him; and he has his real enemies. The old Bogart emerges in some forceful handling of a blackmailer but only when he is forced to act. He confronts Agnes Moorehead as the real killer of his wife and tries to make her confess, but his manner is as much supplicatory as bullying. In her venomous behaviour, Moorehead is the complete opposite of Bacall (just as the two men that drive Bogart – cabbie and crook – are complete contrasts): Bacall stakes her freedom on helping Bogart while Moorehead flings herself to her doom rather than clear his name. Her death is oddly described by Bogart as an accident though it looks deliberate and makes most sense as a last cruel jest on her part. The scene of Bogart finally reunited with Bacall in a sunny Peruvian paradise provides a closing note of happy enchantment to a film that is often overlooked in any consideration of Bogart's finest achievements.

9. GOLD, GREED & MADNESS IN MEXICO

No such problem occurs with his performance as Fred C. Dobbs, the gold prospector of John Huston's *The Treasure of the Sierra Madre* (1948). Despite its reputation as a more serious film, it is far less compelling as a psychological study of the effects of greed than *The Maltese Falcon*: there the falcon was 'the stuff that dreams are made of,' enough to cause men to kill one another; here it is gold, and the point is hammered home rather than allowed to emerge. *Treasure* is too long, too linear in development, too unvaried in tone; it is a film to be respected more than enjoyed, especially when Walter Huston's worldly-wise old-timer tips us off to exactly what will happen when he speaks of the discovery of gold changing a man's soul, even causing him to murder a partner, and the ingenuous Bogart scoffs that little bit too heartily.

But the film's performances are extraordinary: Walter Huston was deservedly nominated for an Oscar and won, and Bogart, in a startling study of disintegration, is at least as impressive though he was ignored by the Academy on this occasion. The part showed Bogart's willingness to sacrifice his image for the sake of a meaty, challenging part. Jack Warner was horrified to learn that his star ended up being killed by bandits and, though the grimness of his beheading by machete was diluted following adverse reaction at a sneak preview, Bogart's support of Huston's stand against studio interference won the day.

Bogart begins the film as a likeable scrounger, cadging handouts from fellow Americans in Tampico, Mexico, and glad to have the opportunity of working on a construction job with a fellow down-and-out (Tim Holt). When the contractor (Barton MacLane) cheats them out of their wages, they catch up with him and Bogart beats him up – but he is careful to relieve him only of what they are owed and to pay for the damage they've caused to the bar-room. This is a little *too* honest considering the provocation, and shows the film underlining the point that Bogart *has* strength of character – though not enough to withstand the corrosive effect of gold. 'He was as honest as the next fellow,' comments Walter Huston at the end of the film, but the bar-room incident shows him a little more honest than average.

Bogart's fertile imagination and immature eagerness are his undoing. He is the first to tire on the journey, though he earlier doubts the old man's ability to keep up with them; he loses his temper, threatening the old man at the very moment the veteran goldseeker has detected a promising site to excavate. Bogart scoffs at the idea of each man hiding his share of the gold they've found: 'What a dirty, filthy mind you've got,' he tells Huston, adding, 'Only a thief at heart would think of an idea like that!' All three of the men show signs of moral disintegration, being prepared to kill the interloper (Bruce

The Treasure of the Sierra Madre (1948): the three prospectors—Tim Holt, Walter Huston, Humphrey Bogart—discuss their forthcoming expedition in search of gold

Bennett), but it is Bogart who succumbs to a paranoiac suspicion of the other two. His mind finds treachery in every suggestion they make, leading him ultimately to attempt the murder of Tim Holt, persuading himself that he'll be killed if he doesn't. That irritable, nervous side of Bogart's temperament is here given full rein as when he is racked by indecision as to whether to bury or leave the body of his partner whom he believes is dead. Only the chilling arrival of the bandits as he lies defenceless at the water hole calms his fevered mind; desperately and vainly he tries to negotiate an escape from their clutches. When Bogart dies, and the gold is dispatched to the wind by the bandits who are ignorant of its worth, the film should end, but rather typically it can't resist pointing out the irony in words from the two survivors.

John Huston won Academy Awards for writing and directing the film. Perhaps he felt that he owed Warners a more commercial picture when he reteamed with Bogart for *Key Largo* (1948) where the dramatic situation was reminiscent of

The Treasure of the Sierra Madre (1948): Bogart played Fred C. Dobbs, a prospector driven to madness and murder by the corrupting influence of gold

90

The Petrified Forest. This time, though, it was Edward G. Robinson's turn to dominate the action as the gangster while Bogart took the nearest equivalent to the Leslie Howard role as one of his prisoners. Though Bogart had his moment of glory as the triumphant hero at the end, his role marks a move towards a peripheral rather than fundamental role in the drama: he later became more of an observer than a participant in films like *Beat the Devil* and *Barefoot Contessa*. In *Key Largo*, Lauren Bacall is also shunted to one side by Claire Trevor's Academy Award-winning portrayal of a drunken, faded gangster's moll.

Like Duke Mantee, Robinson's Johnny Rocco has all the benefit of a delayed first appearance thirty minutes into the film. Before that, Bogart as Frank McCloud has arrived at the small Florida Keys hotel to pay his respect to the family (Lionel Barrymore, Lauren Bacall) of a dead wartime comrade. He soon finds himself one of Robinson's captives. The gang leader is clearly a vicious and merciless figure and it is only common sense on Bogart's part not to provoke him. Yet John Huston and his script collaborator Richard Brooks make a feeble attempt to pump greater significance into a dated (1939) play by presenting Bogart as a man too disillusioned to care about what happens to Robinson or to risk his own life. When Robinson thrusts a gun into Bogart's hand and dares him to use it, Bogart refuses not because Robinson is all too likely to have given him an empty weapon but because Rocco's men would shoot him and, 'one Rocco more or less isn't worth dying for'. He is labelled a coward by Barrymore and Bacall while Robinson is represented as some dark force hovering over American life instead of a dangerous but pathetic dinosaur who doesn't know he's extinct. 'I had hopes once for a world where there's no place for Johnny Rocco', 'Me die to rid the world of Johnny Rocco? No thanks!' – repetitive lines like these fail to shake one's belief that Bogart, whose eyes

91

have been taking in Robinson's every move, is biding his time as any sensible figure would in the circumstances.

Eventually, Bogart starts to intervene, consoling Claire Trevor after she has been cruelly humiliated and being savagely slapped three times across the face by Robinson. Forced to act as the pilot for Robinson's boat trip to Cuba, he has been slipped a gun by the grateful Claire Trevor. He manages to dispose of two of Robinson's henchmen, is helped when Robinson shoots a third for declining to step out and get shot, and waits for the crime czar to show his face from below deck. Even in this final confrontation, Robinson has the dramatic edge. Bogart waits, silent, gun at the ready, as Robinson tries to bargain with him, lapsing into characteristic bravado in the midst of his entreaties. When Robinson finally appears, Bogart expertly shoots him down and has one image, bringing the boat back, to celebrate his emergence as the hero.

Even the romance between Bogart and Bacall is limited by Robinson's dominance of them, and it is very much his film. It is also an example of magnificently accomplished studio filmcraft: photography, sets, music and editing all make brilliant and interlocking contributions but cannot conceal that there is a fatal lack of substance, despite the pretence that it's not just another gangster film.

Bogart's first film for his own production company, Santana, was an absorbing, hard-hitting study of juvenile delinquency, *Knock On Any Door* (1949). Bogart never took any direct credit as executive producer. The name Santana was that of Bogart's yacht, bought some years before, and also that given to the boat in *Key Largo*. Bogart entrusted the direction to the relatively new Nicholas Ray and played a lawyer, ceding much of the dramatic limelight to John Derek as Nick Romano, whom he defends on a charge of killing a policeman. Bogart's Andrew Morton knows the slum environment from his own childhood before he hauled himself out by studying law at night school.

Left: Bogart addresses the jury in *Knock on Any Door* (1949), while his client, John Derek, sits with an innocent look on his face, prosecutor George Macready smiles, and judge Barry Kelley listens

Right: On the witness stand in *The Caine Mutiny* (1954) Bogart testifies as to the circumstances of the 'mutiny' and reveals his mental sickness as he gets carried away in denouncing his subordinates

The film's impact lies in the revelation that Romano *did* kill the cop, despite his pleasant appearance, earnest manner and swearing to Bogart on his mother's life that he is innocent to persuade Bogart to take the case. In court, we side with Bogart helped by the cheap tactics of the prosecuting attorney played by George Macready, an actor with a villainous image whom we automatically distrust. When Macready needles Derek into an admission of guilt (and then disarmingly apologizes for the methods he has been forced to adopt to obtain the truth), the shocked Bogart can only plead for the mercy of the court, blaming Nick's character on society and declaring, 'Knock on any door and you may find a Nick Romano!' But it is to no avail and Bogart is left trying to console his client in the death cell with the promise of making more effort to help others like him.

Bogart's character had rather more complexity than might have been expected. He makes heroic gestures, like ignoring the advice of his employers that taking the case might damage his career, but he also carries a nagging guilt about not having done enough in the past and being too impatient with Nick over his difficulties. Bogart was even given background colour: a happy marriage and evenings spent playing chess. In all, Bogart was playing a more average man that he usually did. The film's stark outcome was to be in line with Bogart's next three productions, all of which carried downbeat endings.

Knock On Any Door was commercially and critically successful but the next Santana production, *Tokyo Joe* (1949), merely made money. The Bogart character, called Joe Barrett, is a Rick Blaine type from the Orient, the proprietor of 'Tokyo Joe's,' a Japanese nightclub, until the outbreak of war when he became a celebrated fighter pilot on the Allied side. Returning to occupied Japan after the war, he is relieved to find that his White Russian wife Trina (Florence Marly) is alive but disturbed to learn that she was forced to make propaganda broadcasts by the Japanese under threat of losing their daughter, and that she has remarried (Alexander Knox). To protect her from exposure and arrest, he agrees to the demands of Baron Kimura (Sessue Hayakawa) and starts a small airline as a cover for illegal activities. The evil Baron kidnaps his daughter to ensure that he smuggles three Japanese war criminals back to their homeland. Bogart turns them over to the American authorities, rescues his child, but is shot. He dies believing he will be able to pick up his life with his wife and child, but this 'tough' ending proved to be too little and too late to redeem a plodding and cliché-ridden narrative.

Bogart was reputedly more concerned with another 'production': his first child, a son called Stephen Humphrey Bogart, born on 7 January 1949. He was later to have a daughter, Leslie Howard Bogart, born on 23 August 1952 and named after the star who had helped him so much over *The Petrified Forest*.

Chain Lightning (1950) is the most negligible of all Bogart's

Bogart and Audrey Hepburn both look unusually solemn in this shot taken during the production of the light comedy *Sabrina* (1954)

later films: it isn't even notably *bad*, just indifferent. Bogart seems to have done it to keep his contract with Warners going (his Santana pictures were released through Columbia). Here he is the former wartime flying ace who finds excitement testing a new jet plane being built by an unscrupulous manufacturer (Raymond Massey). He takes risks for a bonus and turns the test programme into a race that claims the life of the plane's designer (Richard Whorf). He makes amends by successfully testing the ejection seat that killed Whorf and sorts out his romantic misunderstandings with Eleanor Parker. The film is really the *China Clipper* of its time, relying on a topical background to atone for a foreground emptiness.

Bogart's third Santana picture is remarkable. *In a Lonely Place* (1950) takes the violent side of the Bogart persona, detaches it from the usual gangster/crime milieu and relocates it in a stressful setting of Hollywood and the investigation of a murder of passion. Violence as a rational weapon of the professional criminal and a valid one for the hero in a tight spot here becomes an irrational, irresistible force that can destroy an ordinary man. There are no cosy explanations (like wartime experiences or a troubled childhood) to explain Bogart's violent temper as screenwriter Dixon Steele. It is obvious, though, that his contempt for the hack work he has been doing is a contributing factor and the calming influence of a patient and loving woman (Gloria Grahame), who provides a climate in which he can work creatively, makes him happy and peaceful.

Because of his violent past (he broke a former girlfriend's nose in a quarrel), Bogart is a prime suspect when a girl is found strangled shortly after leaving his apartment. He uses his imagination to show a policeman friend (Frank Lovejoy) how the murder might have been committed and is so persuasive that he increases the suspicions of the police. Bogart's manner of lovemaking with Gloria Grahame is also disturbing: when he locks her head in a vice-like grip with his fingers round her neck, he could be as easily going to strangle her or break her neck as kiss her. She tries to make him take a rest from a marathon stretch of writing and he reacts by seizing her and forcing her away – his outburst is a comic one but she is momentarily taken aback and he again indicates how violence is a characteristic mode of expression with him.

Under continuing pressure from the police, Bogart is only restrained by Gloria Grahame's cries from beating the brains out of a boy motorist with whom he has nearly collided on a winding road at night. She inevitably concludes that Bogart could be the murderer and tries to disengage herself from him.

As in other films, Bogart reacts explosively to any kind of deceit. He punches his friend and agent (Art Smith) in the face for a well-intentioned act that Bogart regards as underhand. As in the case of the motorist, he regrets his actions and tries to make amends. When he finds that Grahame has

Tokyo Joe (1949): Sessue Hayakawa as the inscrutable Oriental, and Humphrey Bogart as the pragmatic American

Above left: Bogart, as a neurotic screenwriter prone to violent outbursts, comes under the calming influence of Gloria Grahame in *In a Lonely Place* (1950)

Below left: Later on Bogart apologizes to his agent—Art Smith—after striking him in the face. Steven Geray keeps a watchful eye

Above: In *The Enforcer* (*Murder Inc.*) (1951) Bogart, an assistant District Attorney, arrives to calm a terrified prisoner (Ted de Corsia) making a futile escape attempt

secretly arranged to run off after she has agreed to marry him, he is driven unmistakeably to attempting to strangle her. Only the insistent ringing of the telephone brings him to his senses, just as her alarmed cries saved the motorist. The police find out that Bogart was not the killer, apologize for their harassment, but it is too late: Bogart walks off alone to a very uncertain future.

In a Lonely Place must have disconcerted Bogart's followers by lacking a melodramatic conclusion, especially with a murder investigation to be resolved. The film was too honest, painful and off-beat to fare well commercially. Under Nicholas Ray's sensitive direction, Bogart was stretched further than he was normally accustomed to going: his performance is searingly honest and the film represents one of his finest acting achievements. However, he didn't like it very much, in part because Warners, who had Lauren Bacall under contract, refused to loan her for the role Gloria Grahame eventually played. Warners were piqued that he had

chosen not to release his Santana productions through them.

Bogart's last film for Warners was an excellent one: *The Enforcer* (1951), released in Britain as *Murder Inc*. A cleverly constructed, gripping exposé of an organization in the business of murder, it explained the terminology of 'hits' and 'contracts' and had Bogart as its only star name in a role that didn't really require a star. His part, as the Assistant District Attorney heading an investigation team, is not that taxing nor substantially developed. We never know for instance if he's married, what his interests outside of work are, etc. Showier roles go to Ted de Corsia and Zero Mostel, as terrified betrayers of the organization, and Everett Sloane who is belatedly introduced as its evil mastermind. Bogart subordinates himself to the documentary-like, unemphatic concentration on dogged team investigation for most of the film and is only belatedly permitted to do some solitary heroics. Then we see the old Bogart at a dockland rendezvous with the fearful Ted de Corsia. Later, collecting a vital witness from a telephone box, he spots a waiting killer (Bob Steele) in the reflection of the glass door as he opens it and whirls to shoot him down as effectively as he disposed of the same actor in *The Big Sleep*. This climax takes some contriving: Bogart improbably dispatches *all* the police help in the wrong direction in the hope of drawing off the watching killers, then goes alone to the witness's hiding place, taking a gun offered him by a police captain.

Sirocco (1951): Bogart as a gunrunner in troubled Damascus, with Lee J. Cobb as the French intelligence officer whose courage he comes to admire

Previous page: In *The Enforcer*, Roy Roberts, Bogart and King Donovan survey evidence dredged from a swamp of the victims of the organization that murders by contract

The last fully-fledged Santana production was *Sirocco* (1951) which Bogart claimed was forced on him. Evidently Columbia saw yet another *Casablanca* and sensed big profits; critics recognized the similarities and naturally recalled the original to the newer film's detriment. Bogart is Harry Smith, a man who earns a precarious livelihood in French-governed Damascus in 1925 by running guns to the Syrian rebels. Criticized for his lack of morals and political convictions, Bogart replies, 'I've had them – they're left behind in America with my first wife.' The French, under their intelligence chief (Lee J. Cobb), spoil Bogart's relationship with the rebels and he takes an interest in the Frenchman's mistress (Marta Toren) to get his own back.

Bogart then makes a deal with Cobb: he gets a pass to Cairo and Cobb meets the rebels' leader. Bogart is about to leave when he is asked to help rescue Cobb who is being held by the Syrians. When he learns that Cobb has arranged for his girl to leave for Cairo as well, because he did not expect to return, Bogart is impressed enough to rescue Cobb. In doing so, Bogart is subject to a spot of irony as he is blown to bits by a hand grenade, very possibly one of those he himself supplied to the rebels. The atmosphere of bleak pessimism would have suited many French film-makers (like Clouzot) but seemed completely synthetic when dispensed by Hollywood.

Eleanor Parker was Bogart's romantic partner in *Chain Lightning* (1950)

10. AN OSCAR FOR THE AFRICAN QUEEN

If *The African Queen* (1951) now seems too slight for its high reputation, it still has considerable charm. Though a little too academically assembled, a little too sure of its emotional gambits, leaning too hard on comedy and sentimentality, it nevertheless was a bold piece of film-making, photographed under arduous conditions in the Belgian Congo. Doubles, model boats and travelling mattes are evident but so are the leeches on Bogart's body. These – as director John Huston jested – may have clinched his Oscar for the year's best acting performance.

Though Marlon Brando was expected to take it for *A Streetcar Named Desire*, his disrespect for the Hollywood establishment counted against him, and Bogart, whose anti-Hollywood barbs were more acceptable, won because the part magnified (even distorted) the acting skills he had been displaying for years. Bogart could never have picked up an Oscar as a private eye or gangster: that wouldn't have looked dignified. Like John Wayne years later with *True Grit*, he won not for a characteristically fine and economical performance but for an uncharacteristic, expansive, showy one. Still, he was overdue for an Oscar, and the title of the film that got it for him is not so important.

Katharine Hepburn was no stranger to 'attraction of opposites' casting; probably only Huston's fondness for Bogart kept Spencer Tracy from being used again. The contrast between her character – missionary's prim sister – and Bogart's – grimy, unshaven, gin-soaked, skinny, cigar-puffing captain of a small river boat in German East Africa in 1914 – is cleverly exploited, and *exploited* is the word. Hepburn determines to avenge her brother's death by using Bogart's boat, the *African Queen*, to torpedo a German gunboat and bullies the hapless Bogart into agreeing to her plan. Her ruthless methods of ostracization and gin-deprivation are funny because they'd be unbearable otherwise. Bogart's weaknesses are (according to tradition) sympathetic ones and Hepburn's action of pouring away his alcohol while a hangover incapacitates him from effective protest is one of the screen's most sadistic acts.

Still the liberation of spirits continues in a happier sense when Hepburn lets her hair down and Bogart rises to the heroic demands of the occasion, as well as relaxing enough to imitate the passing wildlife with frantic ear-waggling and armpit scratching.

Though Bogart's Charlie Allnut is a Canadian, he was a Cockney in C. S. Forester's novel and traces of that are more than apparent in both dialogue and interpretation: Bogart's moments of deference to Hepburn seem far more based on class differences and his lack of breeding than anything else. Bogart discards his normal, strong screen image and goes so far in the opposite direction as to appear humble and earnest. The afternoon tea scene is a case in point. Bogart sits,

The African Queen (1951): Bogart braves enemy gunfire to make emergency repairs to a pipe shattered by a bullet as the *African Queen* sails on its hazardous trip across Central Africa

abnormally erect, obviously on his best behaviour with Hepburn and Robert Morley (the missionary), but is embarrassed
by his rumbling tummy. He indulges in a spate of nervous
glances and wagging of eyebrows before milking the scene for
a final (and totally redundant) laugh, saying, 'Ain't a thing I
can do about it,' a slight shrug and a cute look further betoken-
ing his acceptance of his stomach's unruly behaviour.

Back in Hollywood, Bogart tidied up his appearance for the
role of a newspaper editor in Richard Brooks' *Deadline U.S.A.*
(1952). Faced with the sale of his paper to a rival and its
subsequent extinction, he mounts an attack on a racketeer in
the hope of justifying the paper's continued existence. There
was little actual action but reams of talk. One feels that Brooks
was too serious to tell his story as a variation on the traditional
gangster-fighting story, but not skilful enough to make his
story and characters absorbing without such customary
excitements. Bogart's domestic difficulties – a wife who left
him and is intent on remarrying – seem very trite, and too often
he is put on a soapbox to speak out explicitly for a free and
competitive press. Bogart delivers one impassioned speech
memorably well – speaking for the employees and readers who
have rights in a paper as much as the financial owners – and in
fact supported Brooks against 20th Century-Fox's attempts to
remove the argument as too controversial.

Bogart went on to work with Brooks at M.G.M. on *Battle Circus* (1953), a film which dwelled on some trivial romantic complications between a M.A.S.H. surgeon (Humphrey Bogart) and a nurse (June Allyson) during the Korean War. The realistic backdrop of suffering in wartime jars intolerably with the slick dialogue and routine characterizations. Allyson has high ideals which are predictably shattered by her harrowing duties and Bogart clutches the bottle to forget an unhappy marriage and congratulates Allyson on becoming 'a true veteran' when she discovers that wars are senseless rather than righteous endeavours.

John Huston had interested Bogart in making *Beat the Devil*

Battle Circus (1953): Bogart, a dedicated M.A.S.H. surgeon is watched by keen new nurse June Allyson and Sarah Selby (at left)

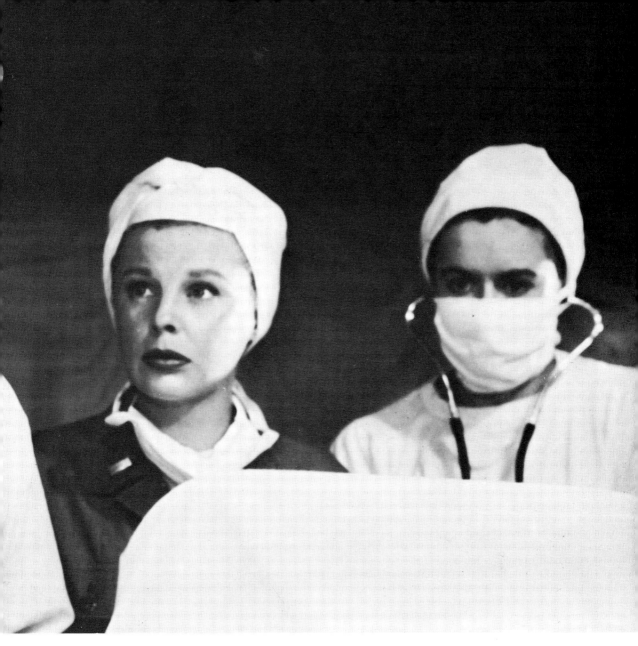

(1953) while they were filming *The African Queen*. The actor bought the original novel and took a financial interest: it was the last venture of his Santana company (although he was not really involved in the production side) and the last association with Huston. In fact, though, the director toyed with the idea of making Bogart his Captain Ahab for *Moby Dick* and in April 1954 was thinking of co-starring him with Clark Gable and making Rudyard Kipling's *The Man Who Would Be King* on location in India. Originally conceived as straight melodrama, *Beat the Devil* was belatedly converted to satire by Truman Capote in a race with the cameras. The result never seems to amount to anything much, yet the film is full of almost

intangible pleasures that linger in the mind. It is perhaps best savoured as a sequel to/re-make of/reflection upon *The Maltese Falcon* (there had been thought of making *The Further Adventures of . . . .* back in 1942).

This, then, becomes Bogart accompanying the Fat Man and friends on another elusive quest for wealth that takes them from Italy to Africa. The international rogue's gallery consists of one English health fanatic and rotund leader (Robert Morley in place of the late Sydney Greenstreet), a skinny Italian (Marco Tulli), a German from Chile with the name of O'Hara, continually mispronounced 'O'Horror' (Peter Lorre, now fat), and a bowler-hatted fascist British major (Ivor Barnard, in lieu of Elisha Cook Jr). Bogart is their front man, Billy Dannreuther, and an amused onlooker. Like Sam Spade, he handles the women: his busty Italian wife (Gina Lollobrigida) and a flirtatious blonde (Jennifer Jones), the spouse of a bogus English aristocrat (Edward Underdown), who lies with the gushing aplomb and fertile imagination of a Brigid O'Shaughnessy, but fools Bogart no more than Mary Astor did.

The film details the comic catastrophes that beset the motley bunch in their attempts to acquire uranium-rich African land on the cheap. Bogart is the only truthful figure among them, so he is naturally disbelieved when he talks of his former wealth. Even he stretches the truth when he promises an Arab

Above: Bogart is amused to find his employers—Robert Morley, Marco Tulli and Peter Lorre—as usual making themselves look ridiculous, in *Beat the Devil* (1953)

Right: Bogart, Peter Ustinov and Aldo Ray made a felicitous team as escaped convicts in the excellent 1955 comedy, *We're No Angels*

110

administrator that he can arrange an introduction to Rita Hayworth and secures the band's escape from his clutches.

Bogart evades the handcuffs clapped on the rest of the bunch by Inspector Jack Clayton of the Yard (Bernard Lee). The jokey use of the associate producer's name (now, of course, the Clayton of *Gatsby*), was repeating a gag of Bogart's: in *In a Lonely Place* the murderer was given the name of that film's associate producer, Henry S. Kesler. Bogart's hearty laughter concludes the film as he reads a telegram from the phoney aristocrat who has outwitted the lot of them. 'Oh, this is the end!' gasps Bogart, and it is. In reality, Bogart was not so amused, claiming that only 'phonies' could find the film amusing and that it was a 'mess' – harsh words for an ingratiatingly different kind of picture.

As Captain Queeg in *The Caine Mutiny* (1954), Bogart had one of the year's plum parts; Tyrone Power would have been the next choice. Having sought to buy the Herman Wouk novel for his own production company, Bogart had to watch the drama compromised by box-office considerations of romantic and comic relief.

Bogart himself was fine as the captain who takes over a destroyer from a slack commanding officer and attempts to run it by the book. Worn out by past stresses, he becomes dogged about small matters of discipline and antagonizes the other officers who resist his plea for their sympathy, co-operation and understanding. He is grimly pathetic affirming that his wife, child and dog are 'rather fond' of him even if no-one else is, but most of the incidents which cause dissension (Queeg closing down a Hopalong Cassidy film show because he wasn't notified of it; searching the ship for keys that might have been made to raid the ship's store for strawberries) seem to have been copied from some service comedy with Bogart taking his part away from Fred Clark or Paul Ford. More astringent handling by director Edward Dmytryk might have countered this impression; but these and other incidents condemn Queeg as a crackpot unfit to command and make any suggestion that the men were not right to relieve him of command (when he seizes up mentally during a typhoon) into a non-starter.

Bogart's key scene is on the witness stand at the court-martial of the officer (Van Johnson) who took over the ship. Confident, eagerly co-operative, Bogart shows Queeg coming unstuck as he wrestles with the contradiction between the glowing fitness report he has filed on Johnson and the verbal declarations that he has made about the man being continually unreliable. When he learns that further testimony is available that will demolish his case, he reaches for the ball-bearings he carries in his pocket and starts to click them in his hand.

In a huge close-up of Bogart's distraught, slackened features, his pent-up frustrations spill out in a set of hostile

Ustinov, Ray and Bogart in another scene from *We're No Angels* (1955)

denunciations of the other officers, then his eyes dart around to confirm that he has given himself away. This distintegration is a little too easily precipitated by Jose Ferrer as the defence lawyer, and one wishes the film, like the play derived from the novel, had concentrated solely on the court-martial, making the audience judge each witness instead of making it plain that the mutiny was justified by letting us directly view each contributing incident.

Bogart had a flattering invitation from Billy Wilder to play a romantic part suddenly vacated by Cary Grant in Billy Wilder's *Sabrina* (1954) (*Sabrina Fair* in Great Britain); he even won Audrey Hepburn away from co-star William Holden and had top billing over them. He plays Linus Larrabee, a starchy businessman who conducts the family affairs while William Holden, as his younger brother, fritters away his life as a playboy. When Holden takes a romantic interest in the daughter (Hepburn) of the family chauffeur instead of the well-connected socialite (Martha Hyer) favoured by the family, Bogart moves in to try and woo Hepburn away. He assumes that the romantic techniques of his younger days will come back, and dons an ill-fitting Yale sweater and sets out armed with a phonograph and an ancient record, *Yes, We Have No Bananas*. The film was the kind of light, frothy drawing-room comedy that Bogart hadn't touched since his Broadway days, and it required no crystal ball to detect that he would end up really falling for Hepburn and finding his love reciprocated.

After this mildly rewarding (and privately acrimonious) association with Wilder, Bogart went to Europe to star in *The Barefoot Contessa* (1954) for another noted writer-director, Joseph L. Mankiewicz; but just as *Sabrina* lacked the caustic

Left: In *The Caine Mutiny* (1954) Bogart's Captain Queeg cracks under the strain of command as his ship is battered by a typhoon

Right: Bogart, playing a sombre business executive, tries to calm Audrey Hepburn as the light-headed chauffeur's daughter in *Sabrina* (1954)

wit of Wilder at his best, so *Contessa* fell short of being a top-level Mankiewicz picture for lack of an adequate story. Hollywood has rarely proved capable of searching self-analysis and films about the film world tend to propagate the myths they are intent on exploding; *In a Lonely Place* is, of course, a powerful exception inasfar as it is about film-making. Here, the dialogue had sparkle but the story was flat.

Bogart was Harry Dawes, an alcoholic writer-director who sobers up to work for a playboy producer (Warren Stevens) and makes a big star out of a nightclub dancer (Ava Gardner). The film opens with her funeral and goes into flashbacks, largely narrated by Bogart who is enabled to fire off such confidences as 'The difference between European and American movie magnates is astonishing – there is absolutely none' and rebuke Edmond O'Brien's sweaty publicist for using a cliché in conversation, 'You're being disloyal, Oscar, you're stealing dialogue from television!'

Bogart is an observer of the main drama, happily married and never pushing his relationship with his star beyond the stage of friend and confidante, anxious to protect her from her wilder urges. When her impotent husband (Rossano Brazzi) shoots her and her lover, he tells Bogart, 'I have known for some time that there was someone; it may be a questionable compliment but I did not suspect you.' So much for the roman-tically rejuvenated image of Bogart in *Sabrina*.

The Barefoot Contessa (1954): Bogart, as film director Harry Dawes, and Elizabeth Sellars, as his wife, watch as the film star (Ava Gardner) embarks on marriage to an Italian aristocrat (Rossano Brazzi)

116

In fact, Bogart was intent on destroying it further by reviving his image as a great screen villain. He made his first and only dramatic television appearance playing Duke Mantee in a revival of *The Petrified Forest* which was telecast on 30 May 1955, directed by Delbert Mann, and co-starred Lauren Bacall and Henry Fonda as the waitress and wandering poet.

In *We're No Angels* (1955) he returned to work for director Michael Curtiz, playing a French convict escaping from Devil's Island as he had done on their last film together, *Passage to Marseille*. But here the treatment was comic with Bogart as a crook, and Peter Ustinov and Aldo Ray as murderers. The story told how the trio, breaking out on Christmas Eve, planned to rob a shop but stayed to sort out the affairs of its dithering manager (Leo G. Carroll) and his family. The convicts are reluctant angels, laying on a Christmas dinner, then remarking through Bogart, 'We'll cut their throats – just as soon as we wash the dishes.' The arrival of the shop's skinflint owner (Basil Rathbone) and obnoxious offspring (John Baer), intent on causing trouble, stirs the convicts into using their criminal skills, helped by a pet viper.

In neither plot nor performance is the film subtle: but the playing of Bogart, Ustinov and Ray is relaxed and they work marvellously well together, not least in conducting a mock trial of Rathbone who arranges his own death (as per sentence)

We're No Angels (1955): Bogart and Aldo Ray watch their convict confrere Peter Ustinov display his knack of opening locks with a sensitive clip of his hand. Joan Bennett is understandably perplexed by the work in progress

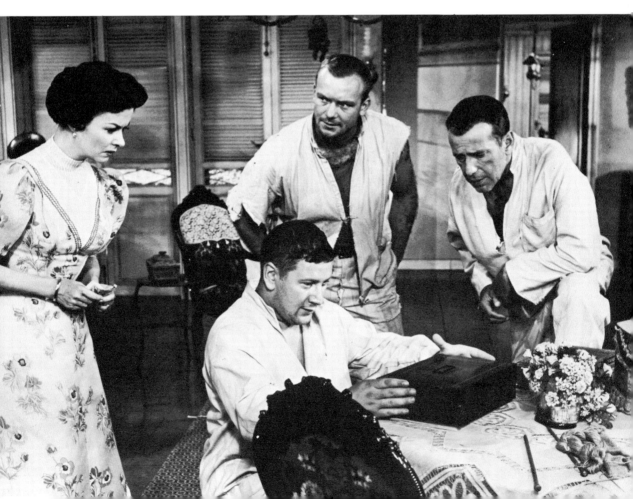

by appropriating the box containing their deadly pet. *We're No Angels* is one of the most consistently agreeable pictures in Bogart's career and one of the more underrated pictures of the mid-Fifties when its modest dimensions counted for little in a period of Cinemascope spectaculars hogging the limelight.

Bogart's first and only picture in that wide-screen process was *The Left Hand of God* (1955), a good example of how dreary films could be unless vigorous direction combated the deadening effect of Cinemascope on narrative pace. True, Bogart has an intriguing introduction as a wiry figure, dressed in black trilby, clerical collar and ankle-length cassock, riding a mule up a mountain trail, incongruously clutching an automatic pistol; but the story soon settled into the routine. Bogart has adopted the disguise to escape from a Chinese war lord (an almond-eyed Lee J. Cobb) and not only maintains it on reaching a mission but comes to be worthy of it by living up to the faith of the villagers. Catholicism was always handled with kid gloves by Hollywood and the milking of the dramatic possibilities has all the usual titillating evasions and senti-mentality: Bogart barely resists the nurse who yearns for him despite the cloth, staring into her eyes trying to remember the last time he walked out with a pretty girl; he amuses everyone with slips that are passed off as unorthodoxy, punching a Chinese in the stomach to make a point about brotherly love, and teaching the children to sing *My Old Kentucky Home* in Chinese, then shooting dice with the war lord for the safety of the village. Bogart gives it as much wry humour as he can, but it should have been another case for Father Bing Crosby.

When William Wyler was planning *The Desperate Hours* (1955), Bogart volunteered to play the part of killer Glen Griffin, who escapes from prison with his younger brother and another convict and terrorizes a suburban household. Wyler was surprised because that part had been played by Paul Newman on stage, but was willing to make adjustments to get Bogart. Spencer Tracy might have played opposite him as the head of the threatened family but neither he nor Bogart would agree to take second place in the billing. Unfortunately, the picture (with Fredric March co-starring) was a disappoint-ment: Broadway decorum and Wylerian good taste sapped the gutsy vitality of a good gangster situation; the ageing of Griffin for Bogart removed the factor of father hatred that had inflamed the relationship with March's character; and Bogart's part was not as strong as it might have looked. He leads the trio of convicts but he doesn't dominate them as Edward G. Robin-son did his men in *Key Largo*. Furthermore, Fredric March's part is built up to make him a character of near equal dramatic weight, more so than Bogart ever was in *Key Largo*.

Among the convicts, Dewey Martin's younger Griffin lays claim to audience sympathy as a likeable kid who went wrong; and Robert Middleton's hulking Kobish takes the initiative

The Left Hand of God (1955): Bogart leads the children in a Chinese rendition of 'My Old Kentucky Home', and (inset) teaches a lesson in brotherly love the hard way

where violence and sadism are concerned. Bogart is unable to restrain his brother from going off or even to divest Middleton of a gun when he gets his hands on one. After Frank Sinatra in *Suddenly* and Edward G. Robinson in *Black Tuesday*, Bogart was really a tame menace. He may down Fredric March with a blow to the head from a pistol butt but he refrains from a second blow because it isn't necessary – thus the film avoids exploiting violence but at the same time makes it less terrifying and weakens the condemnation. Even Bogart's death scene on the lawn when he is riddled with police bullets is handled from a discreet, low angle and allows him only one parting wheeze: a far cry from his deaths back in the thirties. The dialogue is continually trite and forgettable, and the overlong film's only real dramatic asset is a suspenseful last twenty minutes as the police lay siege to the house.

Bogart felt tired during the making of his last film, *The Harder They Fall* (1956), but was too professional to let it show. He played out-of-work sportswriter Eddie Willis who succumbs to bait offered by callous boxing promoter Nick Benko (Rod Steiger) who needs him to help promote a South American ox (Mike Lane) with a 'powder puff punch and a glass jaw' through a series of fixed fights to be a contender for world heavyweight. Thus Bogart smoothly betrays old trusts, wheedles for favours, lies to the press, and soothes his con-

The Harder They Fall (1956): two acting generations meet head on in this, Bogart's last film. Rod Steiger points the finger and Nehemiah Persoff watches

The Desperate Hours
(1955): Bogart as Glenn
Griffin, killer on the loose,
is seen with Fredric
March as the head of the
household that he has
invaded. March comforts
his wife (Martha Scott) and
son (Richard Eyer)

science with small gestures on behalf of the underprivileged
fighters in Nick Benko's circus. Eventually, of course, Bogart
can swallow no more and levels with the duped boxer, rushing
him out of the country and out of Steiger's hands. Steiger and
his men crowd into Bogart's humble apartment and Bogart
announces he will expose the whole rotten business in print.

Here is the narrow-eyed, finger-pointing, now-get-this-
straight Bogart in all his assertive glory for the last time. 'You
can't scare me and you can't buy me and you haven't got any
other way. Nick, you're in trouble!' As the frothing promoter
departs, Bogart's wife (Jan Sterling) pours him some coffee.
He starts hammering the keys of his typewriter. His opening
sentence ends the picture with a startling punch, taking matters far beyond the specific corruption in the picture: 'Boxing
should be outlawed in the United States if it takes an Act of
Congress to do it.'

As editorial cinema, *The Harder They Fall* is exciting but
far from convincing. It is rather more interesting in the way it
catches the collision of two generations: Bogart of the old,
Steiger of the new. Now at least, it is clear that Bogart is the
winner of their big match. He is cool, crisp, concise, while
Steiger is powerful but monotonous and overheated. It is worth
adding that, three years later, Steiger provided an interesting
interpretation in *Al Capone*, further inviting comparison with
the gangster stars of the thirties like Bogart.

121

Bogart next looked forward to making a sea story called *The Good Shepherd* for Columbia with Jerry Wald producing and Ranald MacDougall (who had scripted *We're No Angels*) directing from his screenplay, derived from the C. S. Forester novel; Bogart was to play the U.S. commander of an Allied convoy during World War II. A May 1956 start was announced.

But a medical check revealed cancer of the throat; there was a lengthy operation in March 1956. Press reports referred to a 'throat obstruction' – cancer was a forbidden word. Long sessions of radiation treatment followed. Bogart was forced to withdraw from another film project in July: he and Lauren Bacall were to have starred in *Melville Goodwin USA* for Warner Bros. The roles went to Kirk Douglas and Susan Hayward, the film became *Top Secret Affair* and was a dud.

Rumours that Bogart was seriously ill or dying proliferated during the following months. In October, Bogart issued a statement to the press about 'many unchecked and baseless rumours'; he had had 'a slight malignancy in my oesophagus' and it had been successfully removed: 'I'm a better man now than I ever was and all I need now is some thirty pounds in weight which I'm sure some of you (the Press) could spare. Possibly we could start something like a Weight Bank for Bogart and, believe me, I'm not particular which part of your anatomies it comes from.' Much further jesting decorated the lengthy statement.

It seems that Bogart did underestimate the seriousness of his condition. He had his yacht, the *Santana*, repainted – hardly the act of a man not expecting to use it again. He was regularly contacted by Harry Cohn of Columbia who kept him thinking about making *The Good Shepherd*, cheerfully postponing a September start to January 1957, and then letting the project die with Bogart. For, in November, Bogart returned to hospital for a while. Allowed home, he saw old friends and kept up a bold front. On 2 January 1957, he enjoyed a big fight on TV (there was evidently no personal conviction behind the closing argument of *The Harder They Fall*). The next day, his wife declared, 'Of course he's ill, but he's not done yet . . . I want his friends to know that he aims to be around for quite a while.' But wanting was one thing, the reality another. Shortly after two in the morning of 14 January 1957, Humphrey DeForest Bogart died. At his own wish, there were no flowers at the funeral; he asked for donations to the American Cancer Society. John Huston provided a much-quoted address to the mourners. 'He was endowed with the greatest gift a man can have, talent. . . . He is quite irreplaceable. There will never be another like him,' said Bogart's old friend in part. These words, born out of sadness, have stood the test of time. And the films survive to prove the case. Bogart is dead, but Bogart lives as a notable screen artist.

Bogart Filmography

Key

P	=	producer
Ap	=	associate producer
D	=	director
S	=	screenwriter
Ph	=	photographer
M	=	music
Lp	=	leading players
Ad	=	art director
E	=	editor

1930 **Broadway's Like That**
Vitaphone – Warner Bros. *D* Murray Roth. *S* Stanley Rauh. *M* Harold Levey. 10 minutes. Premiere: March. *Lp* Ruth Etting, Humphrey Bogart, Joan Blondell

Up the River
Fox. *D* John Ford. Staged by William Collier Jr. *S* Maurine Watkins. *Ph* Joseph August. *Ad* Duncan Cramer. *E* Frank E. Hull. 92 minutes. New York premiere: October. *Lp* Spencer Tracy, Warren Hymer, Humphrey Bogart, Claire Luce, Joan Lawes, Sharon Lynn, William Collier Sr, Louise MacIntosh, Edythe Chapman

A Devil with Woman
Fox. *D* Irving Cummings. *Ap* George Middleton. *S* Dudley Nichols and Henry M. Johnson, based on the magazine story *Dust and Sun* by Clements Ripley. *Ph* Arthur Todd and Al Brick. *Ad* William Darling. *E* Jack Murray. 76 minutes. New York premiere: October. *Lp* Victor McLaglen, Mona Maris, Humphrey Bogart, Michael Vavitch, Luana Alcaniz, Solidad Jiminez, John St Polis, Mona Rico, Robert Edeson

1931 **Body and Soul**
Fox. *D* Alfred Santell. *S* Jules Furthman, based on the play *Squadrons* by A. E. Thomas, from the story *Big Eyes and Little Mouth* by Elliott White Springs. *Ph* Glen MacWilliams. *Ad* Anton Grot. *E* Paul Weatherwax. 70 minutes. New York premiere: March. *Lp* Charles Farrell, Elissa Landi, Humphrey Bogart, Myrna Loy, Donald Dillaway, Crawford Kent

Bad Sister
Universal. *D* Hobart Henley. *P* Carl Laemmle Jr. *S* Raymond L. Schrock, Tom Reed and Edwin H. Knopf, based on the story *The Flirt* by Booth Tarkington. *Ph* Karl Freund. *E* Ted Kent. 68 minutes. New York premiere: March. *Lp* Conrad Nagel, Sidney Fox, Bette Davis, ZaSu Pitts, Slim Summerville, Charles Winninger, Emma Dunn, Humphrey Bogart

Women of All Nations
Though Bogart is listed in the cast of this film, he was cut out prior to release

A Holy Terror
Fox. *D* Irving Cummings. *Ap* Edmund Grainger. *S* Ralph Block, Alfred A. Cohn and Myron Fagan, based on the novel *Trailin'* by Max Brand. *Ph* George Schneiderman. *E* Ralph Dixon. 53 minutes. New York premiere: July. *Lp* George O'Brien, Sally Eilers, Rita LaRoy, Humphrey Bogart, James Kirkwood, Stanley Fields, Robert Warwick

1932 **Love Affair**
Columbia (through United Artists in Great Britain). *D* Thornton Freeland. *S* Jo Swerling and Dorothy Howell, based on the magazine story by Ursula Parrott. *Ph* Ted Tetzlaff. *E* Jack Dennis. *Ph* March. *Lp* Dorothy Mackaill, Humphrey Bogart, Jack Kennedy, Barbara Leonard, Astrid Allwyn, Bradley Page, Halliwell Hobbes, Hale Hamilton

Big City Blues
Warner Bros. *D* Mervyn LeRoy. *S* Ward Morehouse and Lillie Hayward, based on the former's unproduced play *New York Town*. *Ph* James Van Trees. *Ad* Anton Grot. *E* Ray Curtiss. 65 minutes. New York premiere: September. *Lp* Joan Blondell, Eric Linden, Inez Courtney, Walter Catlett, Evalyn Knapp, Guy Kibbee, Lyle Talbot, Gloria

Shear, Jobyna Howland, Humphrey Bogart, Josephine Dunn

Three on a Match
First National (Warner Bros.). *D* Mervyn LeRoy. *S* Lucien Hubbard, Kubec Glasmon and John Bright. *Ph* Sol Polito. *Ad* Robert M. Haas. *E* Ray Curtiss. 64 minutes. New York premiere: October. *Lp* Joan Blondell, Warren William, Ann Dvorak, Bette Davis, Grant Mitchell, Lyle Talbot, Buster Phelps, Humphrey Bogart, Allen Jenkins, Jack LaRue, Edward Arnold, Frankie Darro

1934 **Midnight**
All-Star—Universal. *D, P* and *S* Chester Erskine, based on the play by Claire and Paul Sifton. 76 minutes (in Great Britain: 67 minutes). New York premiere: March. *Lp* Sidney Fox, O. P. Heggie, Henry Hull, Margaret Wycherly, Lynne Overman, Katherine Wilson, Richard Whorf, Humphrey Bogart, Granville Bates

1936 **The Petrified Forest**
Warner Bros. *D* Archie Mayo. *Ap* Henry Blanke. *S* Charles Kenyon and Delmer Daves, based on the play by Robert Emmet Sherwood. *Ph* Sol Polito. *Ad* John Hughes. *E* Owen Marks. 83 minutes. New York premiere: February. *Lp* Leslie Howard, Bette Davis, Genevieve Tobin, Dick Foran, Humphrey Bogart, Joseph Sawyer, Porter Hall, Charley Grapewin, Paul Harvey, Adrian Morris, Slim Johnson, John Alexander

Bullets or Ballots
First National (Warner Bros.). *D* William Keighley. *Ap* Louis F. Edelman. *S* Seton I. Miller, based on his story written with Martin Mooney. *Ph* Hal Mohr. *Ad* Carl Jules Weyl. *E* Jack Killifer. 81 minutes. New York premiere: May. *Lp* Edward G. Robinson, Joan Blondell, Barton MacLane, Humphrey Bogart, Frank McHugh, Joseph King, George E. Stone, Henry O'Neill

Two Against the World (Great Britain: *The Case of Mrs Pembroke*)
First National (Warner Bros.). *D* William McGann. *Supervised by* Bryan Foy. *S* Michel Jacoby, based on a story idea (the play *Five Star Final*) by Louis Weitzenkorn. *Ph* Sid Hickox. *Ad* Esdras Hartley. *E* Frank Magee. 65 minutes. Release: July. *Lp* Humphrey Bogart, Beverly Roberts, Helen McKellar, Henry O'Neill, Linda Perry, Carlyle Moore Jr, Florence Fair, Robert Middlemass

China Clipper
First National (Warner Bros.) *D* Ray Enright. *Ap* Louis F. Edelman. *S* Frank Wead (uncredited additional dialogue by Norman Reilly Raine). *Ph* Arthur Edeson. *Ad* Max Parker. *E* Owen Marks. 85 minutes. New York premiere: August. *Lp* Pat O'Brien, Beverly Roberts, Ross Alexander, Humphrey Bogart, Marie Wilson, Henry B. Walthall

Isle of Fury
Warner Bros. *D* Frank McDonald. *Ap* Bryan Foy. *S* Robert Andrews and William Jacobs, based on the novel *The Narrow Corner* by W. Somerset Maugham. *Ph* Frank Good. *Ad* Esdras Hartley. *E* Warren Low. 60 minutes. Release: October. *Lp* Humphrey Bogart, Margaret Lindsay, Donald Woods, Paul Graetz, Gordon Hart, E. E. Clive, George Regas, Miki Morita, Houseley Stevenson Sr

1937 **Black Legion**
Warner Bros. *D* Archie Mayo. *Ap* Robert Lord. *S* Abem Finkel and William Wister Haines, based on a story by Robert Lord. *Ph* George Barnes. *Ad* Robert Haas. *E* Owen Marks. 83 minutes. New York premiere: January. *Lp* Humphrey Bogart, Dick Foran, Erin O'Brien-Moore, Ann Sheridan, Robert Barrat, Helen Flint, Joseph Sawyer, Addison Richards, Samuel Hinds, John Litel, Charles Halton, Harry Hayden, Dickie Jones, Henry Brandon, Egon Brecher

The Great O'Malley
Warner Bros. *D* William Dieterle. *Ap* Harry Joe Brown. *S* Milton Krims and Tom Reed, based on the story *The Making of O'Malley* by Gerald Beaumont. *Ph* Ernest Haller. *Ad* Hugh Reticker. *E* Warren Low. 71 minutes. New York premiere: March. *Lp* Pat O'Brien, Humphrey Bogart, Sybil Jason, Frieda Inescort, Henry O'Neill,

Hobart Cavanaugh, Mary Gordon, Frank Sheridan, Delmar Watson, Ann Sheridan, Donald Crisp

Marked Woman
First National (Warner Bros.). *D* Lloyd Bacon. *Ap* Louis F. Edelman. *S* Robert Rossen and Abem Finkel (uncredited additional dialogue by Seton I. Miller). *Ph* George Barnes. *Ad* Max Parker. *E* Jack Killifer. 96 minutes. New York premiere: April. *Lp* Bette Davis, Humphrey Bogart, Isabel Jewell, Eduardo Ciannelli, Rosalind Marquis, Lola Lane, Jane Bryan, Mayo Methot, John Litel, Ben Welden, Damian O'Flynn, Henry O'Neill, Allen Jenkins, William B. Davidson

Kid Galahad (retitled *The Battling Bellhop* for U.S. television)
Warner Bros. *D* Michael Curtiz. *Ap* Samuel Bischoff. *S* Seton I. Miller, based on the magazine story by Francis Wallace. *Ph* Gaetano Gaudio. *Ad* Carl Jules Weyl. *E* George Amy. 101 minutes. New York premiere: May. *Lp* Edward G. Robinson, Bette Davis, Humphrey Bogart, Wayne Morris, Jane Bryan, Harry Carey Sr, William Haade, Soledad Jiminez, Joe Cunningham, Ben Welden, Joseph Crehan, Veda Ann Borg

San Quentin
First National (Warner Bros.). *D* Lloyd Bacon. *Ap* Samuel Bischoff. *S* Peter Milne and Humphrey Cobb (uncredited contributions by Charles Belden, Seton I. Miller, and Tom Reed, and additional dialogue by Laird Doyle), based on a story by Robert Tasker and John Bright. *Ph* Sid Hickox. *E* William Holmes. 70 minutes. New York premiere: August. *Lp* Pat O'Brien, Humphrey Bogart, Ann Sheridan, Barton MacLane, Joseph Sawyer, Veda Ann Borg, James Robbins, Joseph King, Gordon Oliver, Marc Lawrence

Dead End
Goldwyn—United Artists. *D* William Wyler. *P* Samuel Goldwyn. *Ap* Merritt Hulburd. *S* Lillian Hellman, based on the play by Sidney Kingsley. *Music direction* Alfred Newman. *Ph* Gregg Toland. *Ad* Richard Day. *E* Daniel Mandell. 93 minutes. New York premiere: August. *Lp* Sylvia Sidney, Joel McCrea, Humphrey Bogart, Wendy Barrie, Claire Trevor, Allen Jenkins, Marjorie Main, Billy Halop, Huntz Hall, Bobby Jordan, Leo Gorcey, Gabriel Dell, Bernard Punsley, Charles Peck, Minor Watson, James Burke

Stand-In
Walter Wanger—United Artists. *D* Tay Garnett. *P* Walter Wanger. *S* Gene Towne and Graham Baker, based on the magazine story by Clarence Budington Kelland. *Music direction* Heinz Roemheld. *Ph* Charles Clarke. *Ad* Alexander Toluboff. *E* Otho Lovering, Dorothy Spencer. 90 minutes. New York premiere: November. *Lp* Leslie Howard, Joan Blondell, Humphrey Bogart, Alan Mowbray, Marla Shelton, C. Henry Gordon, Jack Carson, Tully Marshall, Esther Howard

1938 **Swing Your Lady**
Warner Bros. *D* Ray Enright. *Ap* Samuel Bischoff. *S* Joseph Schrank and Maurice Leo, based on the play by Kenyon Nicholson and Charles Robinson. *M* Adolph Deutsch. *Ph* Arthur Edeson. *Ad* Esdras Hartley. *E* Jack Killifer. 72 minutes. New York premiere: January. *Lp* Humphrey Bogart, Frank McHugh, Louise Fazenda, Nat Pendleton, Penny Singleton, Allen Jenkins, Leon Weaver, Frank Weaver, Elvira Weaver, Ronald Reagan

Crime School
First National (Warner Bros.). *D* Lewis Seiler. *Ap* Bryan Foy. *S* Crane Wilbur and Vincent Sherman, based on a story by Crane Wilbur. *M* Max Steiner. *Ph* Arthur Todd. *Ad* Charles Novi. *E* Terry Morse. 86 minutes. New York premiere: May. *Lp* Humphrey Bogart, Gale Page, Billy Halop, Bobby Jordan, Huntz Hall, Leo Gorcey, Bernard Punsley, Gabriel Dell, George Offerman Jr, Weldon Heyburn, Cy Kendall, Charles Trowbridge

Men Are Such Fools
Warner Bros. *D* Busby Berkeley. *Ap* David Lewis. *S* Norman Reilly Raine and Horace Jackson, based on the magazine story by Faith Baldwin. *M* Heinz Roemheld. *Ph* Sid Hickox. *Ad* Max Parker. *E* Jack Killifer. 69 minutes.

New York premiere: June. *Lp* Wayne Morris, Priscilla Lane, Humphrey Bogart, Hugh Herbert, Johnnie Davis, Penny Singleton, Mona Barrie, Marcia Ralston, Gene Lockhart, Kathleen Lockhart

The Amazing Dr Clitterhouse
First National (Warner Bros.). *D* Anatole Litvak. *Ap* Robert Lord. *S* John Wexley and John Huston, based on the play by Barré Lyndon. *M* Max Steiner. *Ph* Tony Gaudio. *Ad* Carl Jules Weyl. *E* Warren Low. 87 minutes. New York premiere: July. *Lp* Edward G. Robinson, Claire Trevor, Humphrey Bogart, Allen Jenkins, Donald Crisp, Gale Page, Henry O'Neill, John Litel, Thurston Hall, Maxie Rosenbloom, Ward Bond, Vladimir Sokoloff

Racket Busters
Cosmopolitan—Warner Bros. *D* Lloyd Bacon. *Ap* Samuel Bischoff. *S* Robert Rossen and Leonardo Bercovici. *M* Adolph Deutsch. *Ph* Arthur Edeson. *Ad* Esdras Hartley. *E* James Gibbon. 71 minutes. New York premiere: August. *Lp* Humphrey Bogart, George Brent, Gloria Dickson, Allen Jenkins, Walter Abel, Henry O'Neill, Penny Singleton, Anthony Averill, Oscar O'Shea, Elliott Sullivan, Fay Helm, Joe Downing, Norman Willis

Angels with Dirty Faces
First National—Warner Bros. *D* Michael Curtiz. *Ap* Sam Bischoff. *S* John Wexley and Warren Duff, based on a story by Rowland Brown. *M* Max Steiner. *Ph* Sol Polito. *Ad* Robert Haas. *E* Owen Marks. 97 minutes. New York premiere: November. *Lp* James Cagney, Pat O'Brien, Humphrey Bogart, Ann Sheridan, George Bancroft, Billy Halop, Bobby Jordan, Leo Gorcey, Gabriel Dell, Huntz Hall, Bernard Punsley, Joe Downing, Edward Pawley, Adrian Morris

1939 **King of the Underworld**
Warner Bros. *D* Lewis Seiler. *Ap* Bryan Foy. *S* George Bricker and Vincent Sherman, based on the story *Dr Socrates* by W. R. Burnett. *M* H. Roemheld. *Ph* Sid Hickox. *Ad* Charles Novi. *E* Frank Dewar. 69 minutes. New York premiere: January. *Lp* Humphrey Bogart, Kay Francis, James Stephenson, John Eldredge, Jessie Busley, Arthur Aylesworth

The Oklahoma Kid
Warner Bros. *D* Lloyd Bacon. *Ap* Samuel Bischoff. *S* Warren Duff, Robert Buckner and Edward E. Paramore, based on a story by Edward E. Paramore and Wally Klein. *M* Max Steiner. *Ph* James Wong Howe. *Ad* Esdras Hartley. *E* Owen Marks. 80 minutes. New York premiere: March. *Lp* James Cagney, Humphrey Bogart, Rosemary Lane, Donald Crisp, Harvey Stephens, Hugh Sothern, Charles Middleton, Edward Pawley, Ward Bond, Lew Harvey, Trevor Bardette, John Miljan

You Can't Get Away with Murder
First National—Warner Bros. *D* Lewis Seiler. *Ap* Samuel Bischoff. *S* Robert Buckner, Don Ryan and Kenneth Gamet, based on the play *Chalked Out* by Warden Lewis E. Lawes and Jonathan Finn. *M* H. Roemheld. *Ph* Sol Polito. *Ad* Hugh Reticker. *E* James Gibbon. 78 minutes. New York premiere: March. *Lp* Humphrey Bogart, Gale Page, Billy Halop, John Litel, Henry Travers, Harvey Stephens, Harold Huber, Joe Sawyer, Joe Downing, George E. Stone, Joseph King, Joseph Crehan

Dark Victory
First National—Warner Bros. *D* Edmund Goulding. *Ap* David Lewis. *S* Casey Robinson, based on the play by George Emerson Brewer Jr and Bertram Bloch. *M* Max Steiner. *Ph* Ernie Haller. *Ad* Robert Haas. *E* William Holmes. 106 minutes. New York premiere: April. *Lp* Bette Davis, George Brent, Humphrey Bogart, Geraldine Fitzgerald, Ronald Reagan, Henry Travers, Cora Witherspoon, Dorothy Peterson, Virginia Brissac

The Roaring Twenties
Warner Bros. *D* Raoul Walsh. *P* Hal B. Wallis. *Ap* Samuel Bischoff. *S* Jerry Wald, Richard Macauley and Robert Rossen (uncredited additional material by John Wexley, Earl Baldwin and Frank Donoghue), based on a story by Mark Hellinger. *M* Heinz Roemheld and Ray Heindorf. *Ph* Ernest Haller. *Ad* Max Parker. *E* Jack Killifer. 106 minutes. New York premiere: November. *Lp* James

Cagney, Priscilla Lane, Humphrey Bogart, Gladys George, Jeffrey Lynn, Frank McHugh, Paul Kelly, Elizabeth Risdon, Edward Keane, Joe Sawyer, Joseph Crehan, John Hamilton, Abner Biberman, John Deering

The Return of Doctor X
First National—Warner Bros. *D* Vincent Sherman. *Ap* Bryan Foy. *S* Lee Katz, based on the story *The Doctor's Secret* by William J. Makin. *Ph* Sid Hickox. *Ad* Esdras Hartley. *E* Thomas Pratt. 62 minutes. New York premiere: November. *Lp* Humphrey Bogart, Rosemary Lane, Wayne Morris, Dennis Morgan, John Litel, Lya Lys, Huntz Hall, John Ridgely

1940
Invisible Stripes
First National—Warner Bros. *D* Lloyd Bacon. *P* Hal B. Wallis. *Ap* Louis F. Edelman. *S* Warren Duff, based on a story by Jonathan Finn from a novel by Warden Lewis E. Lawes. *M* Heinz Roemheld. *Ph* Ernie Haller. *Ad* Max Parker. *E* James Gibbon. 82 minutes. New York premiere: January. *Lp* George Raft, Jane Bryan, William Holden, Humphrey Bogart, Flora Robson, Paul Kelly, Lee Patrick, Henry O'Neill, Frankie Thomas, Moroni Olsen, Margot Stevenson, Marc Lawrence, Joseph Downing, Leo Gorcey, William Haade, Tully Marshall

Virginia City
Warner Bros.—First National. *D* Michael Curtiz. *P* Hal B. Wallis. *Ap* Robert Fellows. *S* Robert Buckner (uncredited additional material by Howard Koch and Norman Reilly Raine). *M* Max Steiner. *Ph* Sol Polito. *Ad* Ted Smith. *E* George Amy. 121 minutes. New York premiere: March. *Lp* Errol Flynn, Miriam Hopkins, Randolph Scott, Humphrey Bogart, Frank McHugh, Alan Hale, Guinn 'Big Boy' Williams, John Litel, Douglass Dumbrille, Moroni Olsen, Russell Hicks, Dickie Jones, Russell Simpson, Victor Kilian, Charles Middleton, George Regas, Paul Fix, Ward Bond

It All Came True
Warner Bros.—First National. *D* Lewis Seiler. *P* Hal B. Wallis. *Ap* Mark Hellinger. *S* Michael Fessier and Lawrence Kimble, based on the novel *Better Than Life* by Louis Bromfield. *M* Heinz Roemheld. *Ph* Ernest Haller. *Ad* Max Parker. *E* Thomas Richards. 97 minutes. New York premiere: April. *Lp* Ann Sheridan, Jeffrey Lynn, Humphrey Bogart, ZaSu Pitts, Una O'Connor, Jessie Busley, John Litel, Grant Mitchell, Felix Bressart, Charles Judels, Brandon Tynan, Howard Hickman

Brother Orchid
Warner Bros.—First National. *D* Lloyd Bacon. *P* Hal B. Wallis. *Ap* Mark Hellinger. *S* Earl Baldwin, based on a magazine story by Richard Connell. *M* Heinz Roemheld. *Ph* Tony Gaudio. *Ad* Max Parker. *E* William Holmes. 91 minutes. New York premiere: June. *Lp* Edward G. Robinson, Ann Sothern, Humphrey Bogart, Donald Crisp, Ralph Bellamy, Allen Jenkins, Charles D. Brown, Cecil Kellaway, Morgan Conway, Richard Lane, Paul Guilfoyle, John Ridgely, Joseph Crehan

They Drive by Night (Great Britain: *The Road to Frisco*)
Warner Bros.—First National. *D* Raoul Walsh. *P* Hal B. Wallis. *Ap* Mark Hellinger. *S* Jerry Wald and Richard Macaulay, based on the novel *Long Haul* by A. I. Bezzerides. *M* Adolph Deutsch. *Ph* Arthur Edeson. *Ad* John Hughes. *E* Thomas Richards. 97 minutes. New York premiere: July. *Lp* George Raft, Ann Sheridan, Ida Lupino, Humphrey Bogart, Gale Page, Alan Hale, Roscoe Karns, John Litel, George Tobias, Henry O'Neill, Charles Halton

High Sierra
Warner Bros.—First National. *D* Raoul Walsh. *P* Hal B. Wallis. *Ap* Mark Hellinger. *S* John Huston and W. R. Burnett, based on the latter's novel. *M* Adolph Deutsch. *Ph* Tony Gaudio. *Ad* Ted Smith. *E* Jack Killifer. 100 minutes. New York premiere: January. *Lp* Ida Lupino, Humphrey Bogart, Alan Curtis, Arthur Kennedy, Joan Leslie, Henry Hull, Henry Travers, Elizabeth Risdon, Jerome Cowan, Minna Gombell, Barton MacLane, Cornel Wilde, Donald MacBride, Paul Harvey, John Eldredge, Zero

The Wagons Roll at Night
Warner Bros.—First National. *D* Ray Enright. *Ap* Harlan

Thompson. *S* Fred Niblo Jr and Barry Trivers, based on a story (the novel *Kid Galahad*) by Francis Wallace. *M* H. Roemheld. *Ph* Sid Hickox. *Ad* Hugh Reticker. *E* Mark Richards. 84 minutes. New York premiere: May. *Lp* Humphrey Bogart, Sylvia Sidney, Eddie Albert, Joan Leslie, Sig Rumann, Cliff Clark, Charley Foy

The Maltese Falcon
Warner Bros.—First National. *D* and *S* John Huston, based on the novel by Dashiell Hammett. *P* Hal B. Wallis. *Ap* Henry Blanke. *M* Adolph Deutsch. *Ph* Arthur Edeson. *Ad* Robert Haas. *E* Thomas Richards. 100 minutes. New York premiere: October. *Lp* Humphrey Bogart, Mary Astor, Gladys George, Peter Lorre, Barton MacLane, Lee Patrick, Sydney Greenstreet, Ward Bond, Jerome Cowan, Elisha Cook Jr, James Burke, John Hamilton, Walter Huston

1942
All Through the Night
Warner Bros.—First National. *D* Vincent Sherman. *P* Hal B. Wallis. *Ap* Jerry Wald. *S* Leonard Spigelgass and Edwin Gilbert, based on a story by Leonard Spigelgass and Leonard Q. Ross. *M* Adolph Deutsch. *Ph* Sid Hickox. *Ad* Max Parker. *E* Rudi Fehr. 107 minutes. New York premiere: January. *Lp* Humphrey Bogart, Conrad Veidt, Kaaren Verne, Jane Darwell, Frank McHugh, Peter Lorre, Judith Anderson, William Demarest, Jackie C. Gleason, Phil Silvers, Wallace Ford, Barton MacLane, Edward Brophy, Martin Kosleck, Ludwig Stossel

In This Our Life
While John Huston was making his second picture as a director, several players from *The Maltese Falcon* – Bogart, Mary Astor, Peter Lorre, Sydney Greenstreet, Ward Bond, Barton MacLane, and Elisha Cook Jr – came onto the roadhouse set and took up positions as extras, apparently being visible in the film to sharp-eyed observers

The Big Shot
Warner Bros.—First National. *D* Lewis Seiler. *P* Walter MacEwen. *S* Bertram Millhauser, Abem Finkel and Daniel Fuchs. *M* Adolph Deutsch. *Ph* Sid Hickox. *Ad* John Hughes. *E* Jack Killifer. 82 minutes. New York premiere: July. *Lp* Humphrey Bogart, Irene Manning, Richard Travis, Susan Peters, Stanley Ridges, Minor Watson, Chick Chandler, Joseph Downing, Howard da Silva, Murray Alper, Roland Drew, John Ridgely, John Hamilton, Virginia Brissac

Across the Pacific
Warner Bros.—First National. *D* John Huston (also, uncredited: Vincent Sherman). *P* Jerry Wald and Jack Saper. *S* Richard Macaulay, based on the story *Aloha Means Goodbye* by Robert Carson. *M* Adolph Deutsch. *Ph* Arthur Edeson. *Ad* Robert Haas and Hugh Reticker. *E* Frank Magee. 97 minutes. New York premiere: September. *Lp* Humphrey Bogart, Mary Astor, Sydney Greenstreet, Charles Halton, Victor Sen Yung, Roland Got, Lee Tung Foo, Frank Wilcox, Paul Stanton, Monte Blue, Kam Tong, John Hamilton, Keye Luke

Casablanca
Warner Bros.—First National. *D* Michael Curtiz. *P* Hal B. Wallis, *S* Julius J. and Philip G. Epstein and Howard Koch, based on the play *Everybody Comes to Rick's* by Murray Burnett and Joan Alison. *M* Max Steiner. *Ph* Arthur Edeson. *Ad* Carl Jules Weyl. *E* Owen Marks. 102 minutes. New York premiere: November. *Lp* Humphrey Bogart, Ingrid Bergman, Paul Henreid, Claude Rains, Conrad Veidt, Sydney Greenstreet, Peter Lorre, S. Z. Sakall, Madeleine LeBeau, Dooley Wilson, John Qualen, Leonid Kinsky, Joy Page, Helmut Dantine, Curt Bois, Marcel Dalio, Corinna Mura

1943
Action in the North Atlantic
Warner Bros.—First National. *D* Lloyd Bacon. *P* Jerry Wald. *S* John Howard Lawson (additional dialogue by A. I. Bezzerides and W. R. Burnett), based on the novel by Guy Gilpatric. *M* Adolph Deutsch. *Ph* Ted McCord. *Ad* Ted Smith. *E* George Amy. 127 minutes. New York premiere: May. *Lp* Humphrey Bogart, Raymond Massey, Alan Hale, Julie Bishop, Ruth Gordon, Sam Levene, Dane Clark, Peter Whitney, Charles Trowbridge, J. M. Kerrigan, Ludwig Stossel

Thank Your Lucky Stars
Bogart was one of a dozen Warner stars who guested as themselves in this musical comedy; he appeared unshaven in 'gangster dress' as a performer in a benefit show who takes instructions from a producer played by S. Z. Sakall. New York premiere: October

Sahara. D Zoltan Korda. S John Howard Lawson and Zoltan Korda (adaptation by James O'Hanlon), from a story by Philip MacDonald based on an incident in the 1937 Soviet film *Trinadtsat (The Thirteen)* by Mikhail Romm. M Miklos Rozsa. Ph Rudolph Maté. Ad Lionel Banks and Eugene Lourié. E Charles Nelson. 97 minutes. New York premiere: November. Lp Humphrey Bogart, Bruce Bennett, J. Carroll Naish, Lloyd Bridges, Rex Ingram, Richard Nugent, Dan Duryea, Patrick O'Moore, Carl Harbord, Louis Mercier, Guy Kingsford, Kurt Kreuger, John Wengraf, Hans Schumm

1944 **Passage to Marseilles**
Warner Bros.—First National. D Michael Curtiz. P Hal B. Wallis. S Casey Robinson and Jack Moffitt, based on the novel *Men Without Country* by Charles Nordhoff and James Norman Hall. M Max Steiner. Ph James Wong Howe. Ad Carl Jules Weyl. E Owen Marks. 109 minutes. New York premiere: February. Lp Humphrey Bogart, Claude Rains, Michele Morgan, Philip Dorn, Sydney Greenstreet, Peter Lorre, George Tobias, Helmut Dantine, John Loder, Victor Francen, Vladimir Sokoloff, Eduardo Ciannelli, Corinna Mura, Konstantin Shayne, Stephen Richards, Billy Roy

To Have and Have Not
Warner Bros.—First National. D and P Howard Hawks. S Jules Furthman and William Faulkner, based on the novel by Ernest Hemingway. Ph Sidney Hickox. Ad Charles Novi. E Christian Nyby. 100 minutes. New York premiere: October. Lp Humphrey Bogart, Walter Brennan, Lauren Bacall, Dolores Moran, Hoagy Carmichael, Walter Molnar, Sheldon Leonard, Marcel Dalio, Walter Sande, Dan Seymour, Aldo Nadi, Paul Marion

1945 **Conflict**
Warner Bros.—First National. D Curtis Bernhardt. P William Jacobs. S Arthur T. Horman and Dwight Taylor, based on a story by Robert Siodmak and Alfred Neumann. M Frederick Hollander. Ph Merritt Gerstad. Ad Ted Smith. E David Weisbart. 86 minutes. New York premiere: June. Lp Humphrey Bogart, Alexis Smith, Sydney Greenstreet, Rose Hobart, Charles Drake, Grant Mitchell, Patrick O'Moore, Ann Shoemaker, Frank Wilcox, Ed Stanley, James Flavin

1946 **Two Guys from Milwaukee**
Bogart and Lauren Bacall made a guest appearance as themselves at the end of this Warner Bros. comedy: she was the dream girl of a Balkan prince (played by Dennis Morgan) but his good fortune in chancing to sit next to her on a plane is dashed by the arrival of her husband, Bogart. New York premiere: July

The Big Sleep
Warner Bros.—First National. D and P Howard Hawks. S William Faulkner, Leigh Brackett and Jules Furthman, based on the novel by Raymond Chandler. M Max Steiner. Ph Sid Hickox. Ad Carl Jules Weyl. E Christian Nyby. 114 minutes. New York premiere: August. Lp Humphrey Bogart, Lauren Bacall, John Ridgely, Martha Vickers, Dorothy Malone, Peggy Knudsen, Regis Toomey, Charles Waldron, Charles D. Brown, Bob Steele, Elisha Cook Jr, Louis Jean Heydt, Sonia Darrin, Theodore von Eltz, Tom Rafferty, Tom Fadden, Ben Welden, Trevor Bardette

1947 **Dead Reckoning**
Columbia. D John Cromwell. P Sidney Biddell. S Oliver H. P. Garrett and Steve Fisher (adaptation by Allen Rivkin), based on a story by Gerald Adams and Sidney Biddell. M Marlin Skiles. Ph Leo Tover. Ad Stephen Goosson and Rudolph Sternad. E Gene Havlick. 100 minutes. Lp Humphrey Bogart, Lizabeth Scott, Morris Carnovsky, Charles Cane, William Prince, Marvin Miller, Wallace Ford, James Bell, George Chandler

The Two Mrs Carrolls
Warner Bros.—First National. D Peter Godfrey. P Mark Hellinger. S Thomas Job, based on the play by Martin Vale. M Franz Waxman. Ph Peverell Marley. Ad Anton Grot. E Frederick Richards. 99 minutes. New York premiere: April. Lp Humphrey Bogart, Barbara Stanwyck, Alexis Smith, Nigel Bruce, Isobel Elsom, Patrick O'Moore, Ann Carter, Anita Bolster, Barry Bernard, Colin Campbell, Peter Godfrey

Dark Passage
Warner Bros.—First National. D and S Delmer Daves, based on the novel by David Goodis. P Jerry Wald. M Franz Waxman. Ph Sid Hickox. Ad Charles H. Clarke. E David Weisbart. 106 minutes. New York premiere: September. Lp Humphrey Bogart, Lauren Bacall, Bruce Bennett, Agnes Moorehead, Tom D'Andrea, Clifton Young, Douglas Kennedy, Rory Mallinson, Houseley Stevenson

Always Together
In this minor romantic comedy, made at Warner Bros., Bogart enacted a parody of *Stella Dallas*, as a distraught father for a film seen within the film by the heroine (Joyce Reynolds). New York premiere: December

1948 **The Treasure of the Sierra Madre**
Warner Bros.—First National. D and S John Huston, based on the novel by B. Traven. P Henry Blanke. M Max Steiner. Ph Ted McCord. Ad John Hughes. E Owen Marks. 126 minutes. New York premiere: January. Lp Humphrey Bogart, Walter Huston, Tim Holt, Bruce Bennett, Barton MacLane, Alfonso Bedoya, Bobby Blake, John Huston

Key Largo
Warner Bros.—First National. D John Huston. P Jerry Wald. S Richard Brooks and John Huston, based on the play by Maxwell Anderson. M Max Steiner. Ph Karl Freund. Ad Leo K. Kuter. E Rudi Fehr. 101 minutes. New York premier: July. Lp Humphrey Bogart, Edward G. Robinson, Lauren Bacall, Lionel Barrymore, Claire Trevor, Thomas Gomez, Harry Lewis, John Rodney, Marc Lawrence, Dan Seymour, Monte Blue

1949 **Knock On Any Door**
Santana—Columbia. D Nicholas Ray. P Robert Lord. Ap Henry S. Kesler. S Daniel Taradash and John Monks Jr, based on the novel by Willard Motley. M George Antheil. Ph Burnett Guffey. Ad Robert Peterson. E Viola Lawrence. 100 minutes. New York premiere: February. Lp Humphrey Bogart, John Derek, George Macready, Allene Roberts, Susan Perry, Mickey Knox, Barry Kelley, Cara Williams, Jimmy Conlin, Robert A. Davis, Houseley Stevenson, Vince Barnett

Tokyo Joe
Santana—Columbia. D Stuart Heisler. P Robert Lord. Ap Henry S. Kesler. S Cyril Hume and Bertram Millhauser (adaptation by Walter Doniger), based on a story by Steve Fisher. M George Antheil. Ph Charles Lawton Jr. Ad Robert Peterson. E Viola Lawrence. 88 minutes. New York premiere: October. Lp Humphrey Bogart, Alexander Knox, Florence Marly, Sessue Hayakawa, Jerome Courtland, Gordon Jones, Teru Shimada, Howard Kumagai, Charles Meredith, Rhys Williams, Lora Lee Michel

1950 **Chain Lightning**
Warner Bros.—First National. D Stuart Heisler. P Anthony Veiller. S Liam O'Brien and Vincent Evans, based on a story by J. Redmond Prior. M David Buttolph. Ph Ernest Haller. Ad Leo K. Kuter. E Thomas Reilly. 94 minutes. New York premiere: February. Lp Humphrey Bogart, Eleanor Parker, Raymond Massey, Richard Whorf, James Brown, Roy Roberts, Morris Ankrum

In a Lonely Place
Santana—Columbia. D Nicholas Ray. P Robert Lord. Ap Henry S. Kesler. S Andrew Solt (adaptation by Edmund H. North), based on a story by Dorothy B. Hughes. M George Antheil. Ph Burnett Guffey. Ad Robert Peterson. E Viola Lawrence. 94 minutes. New York premiere: May. Lp Humphrey Bogart, Gloria Grahame, Frank Lovejoy, Carl Benton Reid, Art Smith, Jeff Donnell,

Martha Stewart, Robert Warwick, Morris Ankrum, William Ching, Steven Geray

1951   **The Enforcer** (in Great Britain: *Murder Inc.*)
United States—Warner Bros. *D* Bretaigne Windust (also, uncredited: Raoul Walsh). *P* Milton Sperling. *S* Martin Rackin. *M* David Buttolph. *Ph* Robert Burks. *Ad* Charles H. Clarke. *E* Fred Allen. 87 minutes. New York premiere: January. *Lp* Humphrey Bogart, Zero Mostel, Ted de Corsia, Everett Sloane, Roy Roberts, Lawrence Tolan, King Donovan, Robert (Bob) Steele, Adelaide Klein, Don Beddoe, Tito Vuolo, John Kellogg, Jack Lambert, Patricia Joiner

Sirocco
Santana—Columbia. *D* Curtis Bernhardt. *P* Robert Lord. *Ap* Henry S. Kesler. *S* A. I. Bezzerides and Hans Jacoby, based on the novel *Coup de Grâce* by Joseph Kessel. *M* George Antheil. *Ph* Burnett Guffey. *Ad* Robert Peterson. *E* Viola Lawrence. 98 minutes. London premiere: May. *Lp* Humphrey Bogart, Marta Toren, Lee J. Cobb, Everett Sloane, Gerald Mohr, Zero Mostel, Nick Dennis, Onslow Stevens, Ludwig Donath

1952   **The African Queen**
Romulus—Horizon—Independent through British Lion (UK)/United Artists (USA). *D* John Huston. *P* S. P. Eagle (Sam Spiegel). *S* by James Agee and John Huston, based on the novel by C. S. Forester. *M* Allan Gray. *Ph* Jack Cardiff. Technicolor. *Ad* Wilfred Shingleton. *E* Ralph Kemplen. 103 minutes. London premiere: January. New York premiere: February. *Lp* Humphrey Bogart, Katharine Hepburn, Robert Morley, Peter Bull, Theodore Bikel, Walter Gotell

Deadline - U.S.A. (in Great Britain: *Deadline*)
20th Century-Fox. *D* and *S* Richard Brooks. *P* Sol C. Siegel. *M* Cyril Mockridge. *Ph* Milton Krasner. *Ad* Lyle Wheeler, George Patrick. *E* William B. Murphy. 87 minutes. New York premiere: March. *Lp* Humphrey Bogart, Ethel Barrymore, Kim Hunter, Ed Begley, Warren Stevens, Paul Stewart, Martin Gabel, Joe De Santis, Jim Backus, Carleton Young, Fay Roope, Raymond Greenleaf

1953   **Battle Circus**
Metro-Goldwyn-Mayer. *D* and *S* Richard Brooks, based on a story by Allen Rivkin and Laura Kerr. *P* Pandro S. Berman. *M* Lennie Hayton. *Ph* John Alton. *Ad* Cedric Gibbons and James Basevi. *E* George Boemler. 90 minutes (in Great Britain: 87 minutes). New York premiere: May. *Lp* Humphrey Bogart, June Allyson, Keenan Wynn, Robert Keith, William Campbell, Perry Sheehan, Patricia Tiernan, Adele Longmire, Ann Morrison, Philip Ahn

Beat the Devil
Romulus—Santana—D.E.A.R. Film—Independent through British Lion (UK)/United Artists (USA). *D* John Huston. *Ap* Jack Clayton. *S* Truman Capote (John Huston was also credited on American prints), based on the novel by James Helvick. *M* Franco Mannino. *Ph* Oswald Morris. *Ad* Wilfred Shingleton. *E* Ralph Kemplen. 100 minutes (UK), 92 minutes (USA). London premiere: November. New York premiere: March, 1954. *Lp* Humphrey Bogart, Jennifer Jones, Gina Lollobrigida, Robert Morley, Peter Lorre, Edward Underdown, Ivor Barnard, Bernard Lee, Marco Tulli, Giulio Donnini

1954   **The Love Lottery**
Bogart made a fleeting guest appearance in this British comedy starring David Niven. London premiere: January

The Caine Mutiny
Stanley Kramer—Columbia. *D* Edward Dmytryk. *P* Stanley Kramer. *S* Stanley Roberts (additional dialogue by Michael Blankfort), based on the novel by Herman Wouk. *M* Max Steiner. *Ph* Frank (Franz) Planer. *Production designer* Rudolph Sternad. *Ad* Cary Odell. *E* William A.

Lyon and Henry Batista. Technicolor. 125 minutes. New York premiere: June. *Lp* Humphrey Bogart, Jose Ferrer, Van Johnson, Fred MacMurray, Robert Francis, May Wynn, Tom Tully, E. G. Marshall, Arthur Franz, Lee Marvin, Warner Anderson, Claude Akins, Whit Bissell

A Star Is Born
'The day that Judy [Garland] recorded the soundtrack for *A Star Is Born* her friend Humphrey Bogart was on the set. As a good-luck gesture for Judy he dubbed in the voice of a drunk in a brief sequence in a café. His voice can be heard calling for her to sing "Melancholy Baby". A stand-in was used in the actual filming but Bogart's voice remained!' (Al Diorio Jr in *Little Girl Lost*, New Rochelle: Arlington House, 1974)

Sabrina (in Great Britain: *Sabrina Fair*)
Paramount. *D* and *P* Billy Wilder. *S* Billy Wilder, Samuel Taylor and Ernest Lehman, based on the play by Samuel Taylor. *M* Frederick Hollander. *Ph* Charles Lang Jr. *Ad* Hal Pereira and Walter Tyler. *E* Arthur Schmidt. 114 minutes. New York premiere: September. *Lp* Humphrey Bogart, Audrey Hepburn, William Holden, John Williams, Walter Hampden, Martha Hyer, Joan Vohs, Marcel Dalio, Marcel Hillaire, Nella Walker, Francis X. Bushman

The Barefoot Contessa
Figaro—United Artists. *D* and writer (also, uncredited, *P*) Joseph L. Mankiewicz. *M* Mario Nascimbene. *Ph* Jack Cardiff. *Ad* Arrigo Equini. *E* William Hornbeck. Technicolor. 128 minutes. New York premiere: September. *Lp* Humphrey Bogart, Ava Gardner, Edmond O'Brien, Marius Goring, Valentina Cortesa, Rossano Brazzi, Elizabeth Sellars, Warren Stevens, Franco Interlenghi, Mari Aldon, Alberto Rabagliati, Bessie Love, Enzo Staiola, Bill Fraser

1955   **We're No Angels**
Paramount. *D* Michael Curtiz. *P* Pat Duggan. *S* Ranald MacDougall, based on the play *La Cuisine des Anges* by Albert Husson. *M* Frederick Hollander. *Ph* Loyal Griggs. *Ad* Hal Pereira and Roland Anderson. *E* Arthur Schmidt. Technicolor. VistaVision. 106 minutes. New York premiere: July. *Lp* Humphrey Bogart, Aldo Ray, Peter Ustinov, Joan Bennett, Basil Rathbone, Leo G. Carroll Gloria Talbott, John Baer, John Smith

The Left Hand of God
20th Century-Fox. *D* Edward Dmytryk. *P* Buddy Adler. *S* Alfred Hayes, based on the novel by William E. Barrett. *M* Victor Young. *Ph* Franz Planer. *Ad* Lyle Wheeler and Maurice Ransford. *E* Dorothy Spencer. Colour by DeLuxe. CinemaScope. 87 minutes. New York premiere: September. *Lp* Humphrey Bogart, Gene Tierney, Lee J. Cobb, Agnes Moorehead, E. G. Marshall, Jean Porter, Carl Benton Reid, Victor Sen Yung, Philip Ahn, Benson Fong, Richard Cutting, Leon Lentok, Don Forbes

The Desperate Hours
Paramount. *D* and *P* William Wyler. *Ap* Robert Wyler. *S* Joseph Hayes, based on his novel and play. *M* Gail Kubik. *Ph* Lee Garmes. *Ad* Hal Pereira and Joseph MacMillan Johnson. *E* Robert Swink. VistaVision. 112 minutes. New York premiere: October. *Lp* Humphrey Bogart, Fredric March, Arthur Kennedy, Martha Scott, Dewey Martin, Gig Young, Mary Murphy, Richard Eyer, Robert Middleton, Alan Reed, Bert Freed, Ray Collins, Whit Bissell, Ray Teal, Beverly Garland, Walter Baldwin

1956   **The Harder They Fall**
Columbia. *D* Mark Robson. *P* and *S* Philip Yordan, based on a novel by Budd Schulberg. *M* Hugo Friedhofer. *Ph* Burnett Guffey. *Ad* William Flannery. *E* Jerome Thoms. 109 minutes. New York premiere: May. *Lp* Humphrey Bogart, Rod Steiger, Jan Sterling, Mike Lane, Max Baer, Jersey Joe Walcott, Edward Andrews, Harold J. Stone, Carlos Montalban, Nehemiah Persoff, Felice Orlandi, Herbie Faye, Rusty Lane, Jack Albertson, Val Avery

Index

Page references in italics indicate illustrations

Short Bibliography

Gehman, Richard: *Bogart*. Greenwich, Conn., 1965; London 1967
Goodman, Ezra: *Bogey : The Good Bad Guy*. New York, 1965
Hyams, Joe: *Bogie*. New York, 1966; London, 1971 and 1973
McCarty, Clifford: *Bogey : The Films of Humphrey Bogart*. New York, 1965
Michael, Paul: *Humphrey Bogart : The Man and His Films*. Indianapolis, 1965
Ruddy, Jonah, and Hill, Jonathan: *The Bogey Man : Portrait of a Legend*. London, 1965 (American title: *Bogey : the Man, the Actor, the Legend*)

Acknowledgements

For their assistance in the preparation of this monograph, the author thanks Pat Billings, Jeremy Boulton, Peter Carr, Peter Emerson, Peter Haigh, Philip Jenkinson, David Meeker, Nicky North, and David Shipman.

Acknowledgement is made in respect of stills, most of which were supplied by the National Film Archive, to the following companies: 20th Century-Fox, Columbia, Universal, Warner Bros., United Artists, M.G.M., Romulus, and Paramount. The colour illustrations were assembled from the Kobal Collection.